Broken Families

*How to get rid of toxic people
and live a purposeful life*

Itayi Garande

**DEAN
THOMPSON**

Publishing

This book was first published in Great Britain in 2020 by
Dean Thompson Publishing

ISBN: 9798698184461

Contents

Bonus chapters

Dedication

This book is dedicated to my mother, Violet, who did all her best to keep her family and friends together.

She also found her calling in looking after many people and helping them to reach their potential, yet she was not always appreciated for her efforts. She, however, continues to live a purposeful life, with no distractions.

It is also dedicated to my wife and children, and to my family members—the ones I talk to and the ones I would love to talk to.

May we all find it in our hearts to resolve our problems with no animosity between us?

In the end, no one will make it out of life alive. We will all die eventually and it would be a tragedy if we leave this earth without giving happiness a chance.

Foreword

There are many things that we need to do to take charge of our destiny. One of the most important things that we have to do is examine the relationships that we have in our lives.

There are nurturing relationships and toxic relationships. Nurturing relationships inspire you. They motivate you and bring the best out of you.

Toxic relationships are relationships with people that always criticise you and always finding fault. All they can do is exploit your weaknesses and remind you of the mistakes you made in the past. These people are bad for your health.

Toxic relationships are more painful and more damaging if they happen to be with family members.

F. Scott Fitzgerald says, *"Family quarrels are bitter things. They don't go according to any rules. They're not like aches or wounds. They're more like splits in the skin that won't heal because there's not enough material."*

This is what makes them difficult to deal with.

Many people put up with a lot of foolishness because they do not have the tools to deal with toxic family members. This book gives you those tools. It teaches that the challenge of growth comes at that time when you are knocked down. Family problems introduce a man or woman to themselves. How you handle your family problems determines how you grow and what you become. You either become evil and obnoxious or you can be triumphant because of them.

Itayi, in this book, makes a very important point: *When you are facing a challenge, the first thing you have to do is evaluate where you are, assess yourself, and assess the situation. What brought the problem in the first place and what was your contribution to it?*

If you do not admit your role in creating problems, you are probably the toxic person that people have to run away from. You will never find solutions to your toxicity and you will never reach your goal.

Earl Nightingale once said, "We are all self-made, but only the successful will admit it." If you admit your role in a problem, you are on your way to personal growth and resolving problems in your family.

In line with his first book, *Reconditioning: Change your life in one minute*, Itayi urges the reader to resolve family problems by *changing their mindset, their belief system*, and the *words they use in conversations*. He also urges the reader to *stop making excuses*, to *become fearless*, and to *find and pursue their purpose in life*.

It is a timely, incisive and relevant book. Every self-respecting person has to read it.

Byron G. Mateusz
Writer and Poet

Introduction

Before you are boxed and buried, decide that you are going to box and bury your fears, your insecurities and your problems by not associating with toxic people. Decide that you are going to live life on a new level, in harmony with your loved ones and serving your true purpose.

Many of us spend a lot of time worrying about things, fearful and not pursuing our dreams. We look for the least painful way to exist. Yet, there is no safe position in life. You can never get out of life alive anyway, so what are you worried about?

You can live your dreams or your fears. There has to be a time when you make that bold commitment that this life sucks and there has to be more to it than these squabbles with toxic family members where you ride together on an emotional Tilt-A-Whirl through Hell. The toxic relative might be fun, charming, the person you send your weird questions to late at night — but they are also a complete drain on your happiness.

You do not need them. Go out and strike on your dreams.

Every day you have to sell yourself and get those old thoughts and old belief systems that cause family problems and limit your potential out of your mind. You have to restructure your thinking, recondition your mind and think new thoughts to confront your problems. You have to get toxic people as far away from you as possible.

Many of us go through life making choices that we think are our choices, but they are not. They are choices that we have been conditioned to make. When we decide not to speak to someone, we think it is our choice. We do not realise that we have been influenced by someone else, by some toxic belief system that we hold, or by some toxic environment we grew up in.

The irony is that we have to design our own belief system, but at the same time, we need other people around us. There is conflict when that happens. We only have enough energy to take us to certain level, so we need handholding from other people, our family and friends. It is, however, necessary that we assemble ourselves with people that share our vision; people that can help us become better versions of ourselves and give us a completely new advantage in life. *These are not toxic people. They are enablers.*

We should not assemble ourselves with toxic people because their toxicity eventually poisons us.

A newspaper article that I read recently concluded that people are dying because of what they are eating. This article was talking about diets. Some inner voice inside me said *even more people are dying because of what is eating them – the toxic relationships that they are keeping and the family problems that they are not resolving.*

When the challenges of life come your way, you have to find ways of increasing your sense of self-appreciation because if you do not do that, you are bombarded with negative stuff every day that eats you down and you will find yourself subconsciously engaging in self-destructive behaviour.

If you do not programme yourself, life will programme you to toxicity.

You need to have an agenda for your life. It is necessary that you do. History is being read, but it is also being written by people with imagination–the imagination to solve problems, to make innovations and to change the world. While this is happening, you are probably keeping relationships and friendships that are toxic.

This book tries to empower you, not the toxic person that has a noose on your neck, to solve your problems and live your life in a purposeful way. This is very important because it takes a lot of financial, physical, emotional, mental and spiritual energy to reach your goal. However, to do so, you have to run with those people who nurture you, not drain you.

You can run faster with 101 people who are willing to go, but you cannot run with one person around your neck. If you run around with losers, you will eventually end up a loser.

My main message in this book is that, in order to deal with toxic people, you have to change, not them.

No matter how people have treated you in the past, if you live with resentment and pain, you are adding to the toxicity that you are trying to run away from. There are no justified resentments in life. You have to let go of resentments. **If you carry around resentments inside you, about anything or about anyone, those resentments will end up harming you. They will create a sense of despair in you.**

I am talking about the person you lent money to and did not pay you back, the person that you feel was abusive to you, the person who walked out on you, and all of the things that you have justified in your heart and in your life that you have to be resentful about. All these things will harm you in the end.

No one ever dies from snakebite. A snakebite will not kill you. You can never be unbitten once you have been bitten. The venom that continues to pour in your system after the bite is what kills you.

ITAYI GARANDE

Other books by Itayi Garande

No. 1 Best Seller: *Reconditioning: Change your life in one minute*

Available in paperback, audio book and on Kindle.

No. 1 Best Seller: *Shattered Heart: Overcoming Death, Loss, Separation and Breakup.*

Available in paperback, audio book and on Kindle.

1. Change your belief system

The difference had to do with was eyesight versus 'mindsight'. Eyesight is limiting; it depends on what you see. It is about judging according to appearances. Mindsight is how you interpret what you see – Les Brown

You probably have experienced many setbacks, disappointments and defeats in your life. Maybe you have already given up or maybe you just need a little fire or a little encouragement to get back on track again. There are things you should look at.

In life, there are winners and there are losers. There are also people who have not discovered how to win and all they need is some coaching, some help and some assistance. They need some insight or a different strategy or plan of action to make some adjustments that will provide a key to a completely new future for them and give them access to unlimited power that they have inside of them. That is all they need.

Think about something that you want for you; something that is really for you, and important for you. Think about something that will give your life some special meaning and power. It could be something that is difficult to achieve; it does not matter. It is very difficult to make the mental leap to understand how you get to where you want to without certain tools.

What are the keys that will help us to discover the secrets to get to our dream?

As a starting point, it is important to say to yourself, 'It's possible.' This simple statement is powerful because it changes our belief system and transforms the way we see each problem and how we deal with it.

When you think about your dream, always say to yourself, 'It's possible.' The way in which we operate as human beings is a manifestation of what we believe and what is possible for us. Everything that you have done thus far in your life is duplication or reproduction of what you believe subconsciously.

Most people operate out of their personal history and out of their memory. They operate based on things they have done, experienced, seen and observed. Yet to live a fulfiling life, they should operate based on a larger vision of themselves. They should see themselves doing what they want to do, not what they are *conditioned* to do. They should see themselves doing something that gives their life some meaning and value.

It is important to operate out of your imagination, not your memory because whenever you look at where you want to be, the default position is to see obstacles to get there, not opportunities. You will hear 'voices' in your head saying, 'You can't do it.' It is important to ignore that inner conversation.

Most people who experience serious problems in life feel that life is supposed to be like that. They cannot see the possibility of life being different. As an example, before April 1954, the universal or common belief was that man was not physically capable of breaking the four-minute barrier. It was believed that humans could not run one mile in less than four minutes. This had been tried many times with no success. Then Roger Bannister—a British middle-distance athlete and neurologist—came along. He broke that four-minute barrier.

Since that time, up to today, over 30,000 people have done it, including high school children.

What changed?

When athletes got on the track, they knew the four-minute record had been beaten before. Because they knew this, they had a new belief about this barrier and about this goal that was previously unreachable. They believed that they could do it as well. They believed that it was possible to beat the record.

The message is: *If someone has made their dream reality, then it is possible that you can make your dream reality.*

As you begin to look at where you want to go, embrace that and tell yourself that *it is possible*. When you change your belief system, you change your life. You can reaffirm this by saying: 'It is possible that I can bring my greatness out here into the universe. I can do what I want to do. *It's possible.* I can write my own book. I can have my own business. I can have a great family. I can mend broken relationships in my family.'

Regardless of where you are in life, you can bounce back in spite of adversity.

I read a story about two men who were working in London City before the Covid19 pandemic. They were high flyers earning six-figure salaries. They both lost their jobs and their families had serious financial and emotional problems. One of the men got discouraged and stayed home watching TV. He became very argumentative and had problems with his wife and children. He got toxic with the rest of his family members. He spent time talking negative to some of his negative unemployed friends. He simply gave up.

The other man kept looking for a job everywhere he could go. Every time he got an opportunity, he kept asking people and checking the newspapers every day for work. He was told, "You have too much education. You're over qualified." He did not give up.

He went to one place and said, "I know you can't afford to employ me but I know you can use my talents, abilities and skills. I don't want to get paid. I just don't want to sit down at home and do nothing. Please let me volunteer. I just want to work. I want to be busy."

The employer agreed.

This man worked hard. He was the first one at work and the last one to leave. He proved himself and became a valuable asset to the company. About four weeks later, one of the top managers contracted Covid19 and died. They were looking for a replacement and the man who was volunteering his time got the job.

What was the difference between the two men?

The difference had to do with what one inspirational speaker called 'eyesight versus mindsight'. Eyesight is limiting. It depends on what you see. It is about judging according to appearances. Mindsight is how you interpret what you see and find solutions to resolve problems.

One man said, *'It's over. It's impossible. I can't do it. I'm finished!'* He surrendered and felt that there were no jobs and life was ending.

The other man felt that, in spite of the nos and the rejection and how bad the economy was and what the newspapers were saying, it was possible. He felt that some organisation somewhere would give him a job. He kept going thinking it is possible. He had a different belief system.

This is what we have to do with our dreams.

It is possible to mend that broken family. It is possible to change the current financial and emotional condition of your family, but you have to change your belief system.

You have to believe that your dream is achievable. Stay focussed on what you want to achieve. Forget the distractions because there are people who make it their business to stop other people getting to where they want.

2. Toxic words

There is no such thing as a perfect family or job security or perfect parent or perfect child. There is no such thing as a storm-proof or tragic-proof life. Life becomes great when we are able to resolve problems, old and new ones.

In life, we use certain words that define our lives. We use words that make us feel like we are sleepwalking through life. They make us act like we are in a trance. These words make us find many ways to cancel out our dreams. One of these words is **but**. **This word is a dream killer.**

There are many things we want to do and many places we want to go to. There are many things we would like to experience and we just stop at *but,* and we build a negative case for not doing those things. *But* is an argument for our limitations and when we argue for our limitations, we get to keep them.

But will cause you to procrastinate. It will cause you to hide behind fear. *But* will cause you to come up with all types of excuses that make you validate your weaknesses and your inaction and not acting on your dream. The word will make you not confront your family problems or adversity.

Right now, more than ever, people need to look for ways to live their dream. People need to look for ways to make it on their own. There is no such thing as a perfect family or job security or perfect parent or perfect child. There is no such thing as a storm-proof or tragic-proof life. Life becomes great when we are able to resolve problems, old and new ones.

There are no guarantees in life. There was a time when we were told to go to university, graduate with a degree, get a job, be successful and then retire.

Special announcement: that day is gone! It is gone and it will never return. Instead of living in fear, stressed out, powerless and feeling like victims, we should start looking at ways to become an active force in our own lives. We should decide to take charge of our own destiny. We should look for ways to design our life of substance and begin to truly live our dreams.

It is time to decide, *'I'll get on with my life, unhindered. Starting today!'*

There are no problem-free moments in life. Soul singer Richard 'Dimples' Fields, wrote a great song called 'If It Ain't One Thing, It's Another'. I say, *"If it ain't one thing, its twelve others."* Always something is there to build a case on why you cannot get along with particular family members, or why you cannot make that phone call and make up with your parent, your sister, your brother, your aunt or your relative. It is usually based on what happened in the past and not what you want to happen in the future.

There is always something that stops you from getting on to the next level and why you cannot manifest your greatness. It is the word *but*. *But* stops you from living life on your own terms. It blocks you, keeps you were you are and stops you from developing your true greatness.

But goes hand in hand with *fear*.

The next chapter talks about how to handle fear and develop great family relationships and personal growth.

3. Hiding behind excuses

Always know that wherever you are with your family, you can enjoy more. You deserve more, but most people go through life quietly, safely, tiptoeing to an early grave. Find out what it is in life you want and go after it as if your life depends on it.

One of the central principles that I live my life with is that, *no one knows enough to be a pessimist about anything.* When we close our mind to what is possible for us or what is possible for humanity, we close off the genius that resides in every one of us. Then we start hiding behind excuses about why we cannot do certain things.

We start making excuses about why we cannot leave certain people or certain situations.

If you are hiding out behind excuses like, *'I don't have enough money,'* or *'I am not cut out for that,'* or *'I don't have enough education,'* take those excuses head on and go and get your life back together.

You are not too old to be loved, to be married, to start a career. Your problems are not so bad that they can never be resolved. Your in-laws do not hate you so much that you cannot resolve your problems with them.

One day I had a conversation with a 47-year-old man who told me that he could not read and write because he had not gone to school. He had given up on learning because of his age and because his sister had been drilling it in his head that he was too old to learn to read and write.

I asked him a fusillade of questions:

'Have you ever heard of adult education?

Have you decided that you should learn how to read and write?

Why do you not want to expand your world?

Why are you using that as a racket?

Why don't you decide now that you are going learn to read and expand your world? If other people can learn, you can learn too.

Have you sat in a class yet? Have you signed up yet?'

He replied, 'No I haven't.'

Many people say no to things. Yet, they do not even know what they are saying no to. This man had never challenged himself to learn how to read or write. He spent his entire life trying to play a whole con game, pretending he knows how to do something that he does not know. Most of us go through life like that.

We go through life pretending. We pretend that we are satisfied with where we are in life. We pretend that everything is okay. We pretend that we do not have any special goals and desires, when deep down inside, we do really want more.

We spend time pretending that we are happy not talking to our family member, but deep down we are being worn down and depressed by the separation.

We want more, but if you look at our behaviour, it tells a different story, a true story about our insecurities and our pain. *You have to judge a tree by the fruit that it bears and not by the fruit that it talks about.* Many people pretend that they want more out of life, but all you have to do is watch their actions. The actions will tell you something else.

I used to pretend that I wanted to lose weight, but how could you tell I was pretending? I would drive by KFC every day from work and have a Tower Zinger burger and a large coke. Watching what I ate would tell you how pretentious I was. I was weak-willed to lose weight, but I wanted the world to know I was committed.

When people were confronting me about problems I was having with my siblings, I always used to pretend that I was doing my best to resolve the problems, but I was doing nothing about it.

Watch people's actions and soon you realise that their whole life is a con. If you think about something that you want to do, like resolving a bad relationship with your sibling, take it head on. Do not pretend. Decide that you are going to start looking at ways to resolve it, go for counselling together, find common ground and resolve it. Explore the possibilities that lead you to resolving that conflict, so that you begin to make that important connection with your family member.

Decide that you are going to face the problem. No matter what shortcomings you have, decide that you are going to strengthen your mind and your resolve. **Start right now.**

American scientist George Washington Carver would say, *'Do what you can, where you are and with what you have!'* George Dudley always talks about always trying to be more than that which you are. Do not be satisfied with yourself because life is always in motion.

Always know that wherever you are with your family, you can enjoy more. You deserve more, but most people go through life quietly, safely, tiptoeing to an early grave. Find out what it is in life you want and go after it as if your life depends on it.

Why?

Because life does depend on it. People who have found their passion, who have found the things they love, who have found the things that they can pour their lives into, live longer than those who have not.

I asked one law lecturer how he had managed to write 40 books, maintain a healthy family relationship and travel the world. He answered, "The kind of work I get to do is *in me*. I never imitate anyone. I live what's *in me*."

I think that is everybody's desire in life. You have to live what is *in you*. Life is too short and unpredictable to waste away fighting with your loved ones and battling with a career that is not *in you*.

Do not hide behind excuses to lengthen the time that you are not talking to your family member. There are no guarantees that your sister or your brother that you are not talking to today will show up tomorrow. There are many people who were here yesterday, that are not here today. Many opportunities were here yesterday, but they are not here today.

You can wait, but Abraham Lincoln said, *"Good things might come to those who wait, but only those things that are left over by those who hustle!"* So who wants to go through life picking up leftovers? You deserve much more than that.

So face your family problems head on and start living life and not picking up leftovers. There is room for you out here in the arena called life to enjoy more, to achieve more, to come out and live your dream together with your loved ones. Do not allow excuses to keep you in the corner, looking at life as a spectator and not being a participant.

All of us showed up in life to give something and nobody is going to give that service that you have to give. No one is going to produce your product. No one is going to write your book. No one is going to open your academy to train people. No one is going to create your day care with a special curriculum to help to cultivate the high self-esteem in our children. *That is your idea and if you do not bring out your idea, when you die all of us will suffer because we have been deprived of your genius.* You allowed excuses to stop you from pursuing your greatness.

Most people take their greatness to the grave. Benjamin Franklin, one of the Founding Fathers of the United States, said, "Most people die at 21 and don't get buried until they are 65." They are walking dead. You can tell by the way they walk and how they look in the face when they speak to you. They have no energy, no zest for life and no motivation.

They have more excuses than actions. They have excuses for everything.

4. Fear

We give permission to our fear to immobilise us. Whatever discomfort, difficulties and challenges you experience exist because you give them permission to exist.

In life, *you can either live your dreams or live your fears.* We all have fears. We all have something that is blocking us and holding us back. As we begin to look at life, we begin to realise that the reason that most people are not living their true potential and not doing all the things that they would like to do is because of *fear.*

Some people describe fear as an acronym standing for **False Evidence (or Expectations) Appearing Real**.

I remember as a child we used to watch horror programmes on TV. There was one particular series called Hammer House of Horror. It used to give me so much fright. I would be scared to move out of the living room into my bedroom. I would imagine being attacked by one of the killers in the series.

Most people go through life running scared of things that do not exist physically, but intimidate them only in their imagination. Yet the things they fear are simply *false expectations appearing real.* We are brilliant enough to scare ourselves to death.

There are people who actually get a kick out of scaring themselves to death. When I watched the crime series, "Crimewatch" on TV, I would come before sunset every day, thinking the crooks I had seen on Crimewatch would attack me.

What are things that are keeping you from confronting the challenges in your family, the problems that are wearing you down? Do you fear the backlash from your mother, sister, brother or cousin if you try to talk about your problems? Is this fear real of it is a just false expectation *appearing real?*

Abraham Maslow said that life is about growth. You can go back to your comfort zone where you will not find any growth or you must be willing to go forward and face your fears again, and again, and again. You are never going to have a fear-free existence. Some fear is acceptable and legitimate. There are things you should *really* be afraid of, but do not allow them to immobilise you. You acknowledge those things, consider them and carry yourself accordingly. There are times that we should proceed with caution.

There is a difference between *having a fear* and *fear having you.* When you have legitimate fear, embrace it, deal with it, and move on because *what you resist will persist*. If you resist confronting your family member about an issue that has caused division in the family, it will not go away by resisting talking to them. In fact, not talking to your family member will make the problem persist.

One thing you will find out when you face your fears is that the situation is not as bad as you think it is. We have had occasions when we faced our fears, got through them and we did not die.

I deal with my fears by imagining the worst-case scenario. When I go to the dentist, I imagine losing all my teeth. When I get my teeth cleaned, I feel like I have achieved my goal because the situation would be much better than I imagined.

Another technique is to visualise myself as being more than capable of handling the problem. So when I have to deal with difficult family issues, I consider myself an expert on the issue. This involves seeing oneself as being worthy, being capable and having what you need to make you a worthwhile person that deserves to be listened to. You have to see it in your mind's eye, confronting your fears and handling them properly.

You have to ask yourself the following questions:

What fears am I holding on to?

What fears am I allowing to imprison me, that are keeping me from living up to my true potential?

What fears are keeping me from really being happy?

What fears are keeping me having a sense of adventure and excitement in my life?

What fears are keeping me from controlling my destiny?

We give permission to our fear to immobilise us. Whatever discomfort, difficulties and challenges you experience exist because you give them permission to exist. You have the power to resolve any issue, but you allow your fear to interfere with your judgment. You are strong enough to do it, and your life is worth whatever you have to go through to get past your fears of confronting your family member. Otherwise, you will not reach your potential if your family problems are a noose around your neck.

Will it be easy to just run out there and do it? **No!**

Will it happen overnight? **No!**

Will it be a struggle? **Yes!**

Will there be times when you cannot make ends meet?
Yes
Will you have some opposition? **Yes, definitely**

So, from this point onwards, mend your family problems by accepting fear as a fact, not as a force.

Accept it as something that you will experience, but something that will never be a force to hold you back. It does not have any special power other than that which you give it.

You accept the fact that you are afraid, and then you move on anyhow. You move on past it and then you do what you have to do.

5. Sitting on your purpose

You can use your beliefs and thoughts as a blocker or as building blocks to pursuing your true purpose.

Many of the problems we witness in families are caused by people who do not have a true appreciation of who they are. That person may be you, the reader, your wife or husband, your parent, your sister, your brother or your relative. Lack of that appreciation and understanding of oneself, makes you abuse and immobilise yourself. You become toxic to yourself and those around you.

You begin to sabotage your life, your dreams and unconsciously begin to work against yourself. You become your own worst enemy.

You can only break away from this self-sabotage when you start viewing your hunger to achieve your dreams begins to move you away from your fear and give you a special drive. You have to work at identifying your true purpose, your true identity and the true power that you have—the true capacity that you have to bring about change. This capacity is the *miracle-working power that you have within yourself.*

A western man was able to live among the most dangerous tribes in the Himalayas, in spite of not being able to speak the language the tribesmen spoke. When asked how he managed to do that, he answered, "When life stops threatening you with death, what else is there?"

The majority of the fears that we have are not life or death fears. They are not that kind of fears. Through our imagination, we blow them out of proportion and give them more power than they actually have or deserve. We permit them to govern our lives. We permit them to stop us from pursuing our purpose in life and to determine how far we can stretch out and forgive our family members for their indiscretions.

Ask yourself whether the problem you have with your family member is something that is very difficult and if it threatens your life. You may be shocked that you are fuelling it by your imagination.

What kind of things or thoughts are you feeding your consciousness?

What kinds of things are you putting in your mind, that will enable you to either move forward or justify why you are static and staying where you are?

Are these things making you sit on your purpose?

My friend told me that he was failing to lose weight because he was 'big boned'. I have never seen a fat skeleton before. Have you? It is his limiting thoughts and beliefs that are blocking his purpose.

You can use your beliefs and thoughts as a blocker or as building blocks to pursuing your true purpose. You can use your beliefs and thoughts to feel **powerful** or **powerless.** Some people are moving on their own, resolving family problems and serving their true purpose because they feel within themselves that they have what it takes to make it. They are not afraid about tomorrow because of how they see themselves and what their purpose is. They feel that they deserve to create something bigger than themselves. These people have decided, as they look at the future and look at themselves, that there is a way to achieve their purpose.

Where there is a will, there is a way. They have the kind of consciousness that tells them to create a way out of nowhere. When you have that kind of spirit, nothing can stop you. Nothing!

What will your life be like, as you look towards the future, if you decided, I'm not going to allow my beliefs, thoughts and fears to stop me from serving my true purpose?

What will your life be like? What will your future be like, if you decided to go after that which you desire so strongly that it prepares you past your fears?

Author Susan Jeffers wrote and amazing book called, 'Feel the Fear and Do It Anyway: Dynamic Techniques for Turning Fear, Indecision, and Anger into Power, Action, and Love'. Through the process Susan has laid out, she makes people discover that fear is simply an unpleasant fact, and should never be a barrier to success. You have to know your true purpose in order to resolve your family problems.

Susan says you acquire a higher level of consciousness that helps your find your true purpose and resolve your family problems by letting go of negative programming, raising your level of self-esteem, becoming more assertive, and creating more love, trust, and enjoyment in your life.

We all have a capacity to resurrect ourselves, resurrect our dreams, find our true purpose and create harmony with our family members. Be willing to learn, to reach out to someone who can help you. Be willing to find someone to hold your hand, to take you to the next stage.

6. Change your paradigm

It is not just because you are lazy. It is because the move challenges your very existence and your identity. You want things that you are familiar with because you cannot stand the reaction of those who always criticise you.

I s your family stuck in a rut and cannot get up? Are you circling round and round the same problem, blaming each other for the dysfunction? You have probably gone up and down the problem mountain several times and are beginning to feel exhausted by the problems and challenges that you are facing in your family. You are almost giving up or giving in.

This is wrong.

There are ways to resolve the challenges and these are internal, not external. You cannot change the other person. You can only change yourself and that change can help others to change.

Oftentimes we try to change the world around us, our family members and our friends, while remaining the same. That is impossible. Sometimes we feel like we are making progress, expanding our horizons and our awareness, but with no real change in our lives.

Sometimes we fool ourselves that we have the desire to change, but we end just there–at the desire stage; the stage of doing little or nothing to change. This is because we get an imprint from society telling us how things are done. If we do not follow what society demands, we feel like failures.

Sometimes it is miseducation. We are taught how to do certain things, how to behave in certain situations, and worse, how to respond to certain types of behaviours. This conditioning brings no change. In fact, it makes us slave to society. The mind has to influence reality if real change is to take place.

Everyone has a paradigm that defines his or her reality. This paradigm is created, largely, by society. So it is limited because it does not include our mind and soul's desires. The tragedy is that many people cannot see beyond their paradigm. They wake up, go to work, get paid at the end of the month, get stressed by bills, ask for help from friends and family, and if not supported blame the family for their troubles.

A paradigm is your reality, but not *the* reality. Your paradigm determines your behaviour, your beliefs and your experience. Yet outside your present paradigm are rich gifts of possibilities to be explored. There are possibilities to be enjoyed and cherished. If you stay in your own paradigm, you do not enjoy these possibilities.

In this book, I try to demonstrate using some stories of real people that if you step outside of your paradigm, outside of your own circle of family and friends, and look deep into your mind and soul, you experience an awakening that shows you many other possibilities. You start seeing things that you never knew existed.

Once you have this awakening, you realise that what you call family problems are just misunderstandings brought by your limited paradigm and the limited paradigm of your family members. You all have a limited understanding of the reality around you.

The mind is rich with possibilities for fulfilment, but you decide to dwell on the limited horizons and paradigms that you are used to, the societal imprint. You do not tap into exactly what your mind and your soul wants, so you live the life that is imposed on you, not the life that you are meant to live. You live the life of pleasing others, life of seeking acceptance not fulfilment.

The number one skill we can ever acquire is the ability to use our mind to create possibilities for our lives, and to resolve problems. This is very important because without the control of our mind, we follow other people's minds and actions, and not ours. Then we fall and we fail. To flourish and triumph, our minds have to really transform and influence our reality. We have to make real, not cosmetic, change.

Many people say, 'I have changed,' but eventually they go back to the same old stuff that they are used to. They revert to original settings after little minor changes because the conditioning is very strong. Conditioning stops true change. True change is not about just attracting new things and ways of doing things, but it is about evolving and breaking old habits so that you can transform. You evolve into who your soul desires you to be. This major shift changes everything, not just what you eat or how you dress, but your relationships, your goals and your plans.

It also changes what you want. You mature and your perception of your wants changes. So you do not just say I want a good relationship. That is an immature want. You say, *'I am going to change today and I will not let anything or anyone stand in my way to get a good relationship. I will be out there looking for greatness and I will not compromise on my needs and desires.'* This is mature wanting.

Mature wanting is knowing what your soul wants you to have–not what you friend, mother, father, brother, sister, friend, work colleague, church member, or community member want you to have. You have to meet your *future self*, if you are to have infinite possibilities in your life.

The problem is that we want what we are conditioned to have, not what our soul wants us to bring to our lives. We all have an inner compass that can tell us what our soul wants, our yearning. We should always check in and find out what that compass is saying before we succumb to pressure.

Your whole life should be about expanding your horizon, shifting the status quo, and exploring infinite possibilities, not just adjusting to what you already found in the world when you were born. If you adjust to what the world offered you, you are wasting the gifts, the capacities and the strengths that are within you. They remain latent and dormant.

You are not here for that.

You are on earth to express greatness in your form, not anyone else's. You are born for a reason. You have to find out what that reason is. This is not easy because you have to dig deep into your mind and soul to know your true purpose. Sometimes that creates a misalignment with those you love; it creates family problems.

For instance, if you truly and honestly believe that you are better off as a single parent, society will put a mark on you; your parents will say things to you; but deep down you will feel that your soul wants that. Societal pressure moves you away from what your soul desires. You are compared to other people, other situations and other relationships. You react because there is a conflict between what your soul desires and what society desires for you.

There are people who need to deal with problems that they have experienced in their lives before, so that they can change reality and expand their paradigm. I am talking about people who need healing first before they can move on.

First, whenever we evolve, the problems we have at one level of consciousness do not exist at the next level. They are no longer problems at the higher level of awareness. When we evolve and move to a higher level, the issue is healed.

A woman who was abused when she was a stay-at-home mother by a man who was a breadwinner cannot remain in the old lower level of consciousness when she finds a career. The fact that she has found a career means she is on a different level of consciousness and can no longer live at the benevolence of an abusive man. She has many possibilities now and ahead of her.

Looking back at the abusive relationship takes her back to a lower level of consciousness and retards her progress.

A friend of mine who had been abused by her husband told me how she transformed simply by replacing the picture of her ex-husband that was on the wall by a picture of her child. I said to her she had replaced the old with the new and had opened up future possibilities. Attention had to shift so that barriers could be broken. When she shifted attention, she healed herself and her ex-husband and now they are raising their child more amicably and have a better relationship than before.

This story is important in highlighting that happiness comes from within us. If you evolve and shift, your life changes. Internal shift, therefore, is important. Your life purpose may not be something that you see right now, but you may never see it if you do not shift your mindset.

The problems that you have in your life right now, with your family, are caused by not having clarity of purpose. If you know your purpose, you start finding ways to resolve what seems like family problems. This book will try to help shift your mindset so that you can be on that important road to mending those difficult family feuds.

7. A hostile universe

Living your dreams, changing your behaviours and overcoming negative habits is challenging. However, when you change the way you look at things, the things you look at change.

Albert Einstein once observed that the most fundamental and major decision that you have to make in your life is this, **"Do I live in a friendly or hostile universe?"**

Do you live in a universe that is filled with hostility and anger where people hate each other and kill each other? When you see the world that way that is exactly what you will create for yourself. This reasoning is from some great scientific minds and the interesting thing is that this is not just a clever play on words.

Imagine the following scene. You are in your house. You have your car keys in your hand. The lights go out because of power failure and you cannot see a thing. You stumble around in your living room and you drop your keys. You look around for a moment and you realise that you are never going to find them in the dark.

You look outside and you notice that the streetlights are on. In your mind, a light bulb goes off and you say to yourself: *I'm not going to sit around here in the dark and grope around looking for any keys when there is a light on outside. I'm going to go out there under the street lights and I'll look for my keys.*

You go outside and start groping around, looking for your keys. Your neighbour comes along and says, "What happened Maya?"

"Well, I dropped my keys," you say.

"I'll help you look for them."

The two of you are now out there looking for keys.

Finally, after a while, your neighbour says, "Excuse me! Where did you drop your keys?"

"Well um... I dropped them in the house," you say.

"You mean to tell me that you dropped your keys in the house and you're looking for them out here in the street lights? It doesn't make sense," says your neighbour.

You say, "It doesn't make any sense to grope around in the dark when there's light out here," you retort.

You may laugh and think this was a silly move to make, but is that not what we do when we have a problem, a difficulty or a struggle that is located inside our mind? **We look for the solution outside our mind, some place outside of ourselves.**

This scenario is similar to a doctor giving a prescription for your ailment to your father, your mother, your sister or your brother and not to you. Yet you are the one with the ailment.

So if you are the one with the struggles and the difficulties in life, you have to look inside and change. Expecting somebody else to change, or something outside of you to get better, in order for you to make your life work, is something you really have to take a hard look at.

Do not accept living in a known hell and not seek unknown heavens. Many people prefer known hells than unknown heavens because known hell is comfortable.

I read a story by Dr Johnny Coleman talking about a man who was captured behind enemy lines in the war and was sentenced to be killed or to choose another option.

They said to him, "Tomorrow you can face the firing squad or go over this door here."

He asked, "What is behind that door?"

They said, "No one knows. All we can tell is that there are just unknown horrors."

He thought about it and the next morning he selected the firing squad. After the shots rang out, the captain's secretary said, "What's behind that door?"

The captain said, "Freedom!"

However, no one would select the door because his or her fate behind the door was unknown. You see, people never live their dreams. They stay in relationships where they are miserable, trudging through family problems saying *they are normal.*

People stay in jobs they hate and take out their frustrations on their loved ones at home. If your work is causing you anxiety and frustration, you are likely to be unhappy at home or living within a broken family.

If your job is making you sick, eventually your relationship will be 'sick' too. You will eventually be in a relationship where you are dying together, rather than growing together, expanding and enjoying life together. Many of us are miserable because we do not have the courage to see ourselves beyond that relationship that has turned toxic.

This is an expensive life, not in monetary terms, but in emotional terms. The price of living your life is not that expensive. Living the truth is not expensive. It is fun. You have to decide which of these two lives you want: Heaven or hell.

People say, 'I have failed in mending the relationship.' *There is a difference between failing and being a failure.* If you try living in Heaven and do not produce results, that is fine, but do not confuse who you are with the results that you produce. The results that you produce can be changed.

If you lose a debate, you lose because of what you do not know, so you can do your homework and get better. The more you do your homework, the better version of yourself you become.

You can either live your dreams or your fears.

8. Know yourself

Wisdom starts when you know yourself. You will realise that everything aligns itself perfectly when you live your truth, break limiting habits and challenge yourself daily.

Many people want to change the world, their communities, their families, friends and peers while they *themselves* remain the same. This is ...p......le. Do you know who you are? If you do not like the results you are getting in your life, *you* have to change. No one else has to change, except you.

You have to dare to be yourself, however frightening or strange that self may prove to be. True belonging only happens when we present our authentic, imperfect selves to the world. Our sense of belonging – to our families and communities – can never be greater than our level of self-acceptance. This means we can never resolve any problem with our family members if we do not know ourselves first.

Most people do not really know who they are. They really don't. When people ask you who you are, you say, "I am John," "I am Sarah," "I am Simba." Referring to your physical characteristics, you say, "This is my arm," "This is my head." However, beyond these responses, many people do not know who they really are and this lack of self-knowledge has caused many problems in life, including many family problems.

We live simultaneously on three planes of understanding. We are *spiritual creatures*. We have an *intellect*, and we have *physical bodies*. However, we lack understanding or awareness of who we are because we are totally locked into a physical world and we let things outside of us control us.

Ninety-five percent of the world population is reacting to life, but not really living at all. This is a barrier to success; but we have to understand what success is first. Earl Nightingale in the book, *The Strangest Secret* says a person is successful if they know who they are, where they are, where they are going, and are progressively moving in that direction.

Success is, therefore, is about knowing yourself and the progressive movement towards a worthy ideal. Anyone who has a goal and they are moving towards it, is successful. Most people think they are successful when they have a lot of money. That is not quite true. Mother Teresa did not have a lot of money, but she was a very successful woman. Many great thinkers and inventors died poor, but they were successful in inventing the things that make our lives convenient today.

There are two barriers to success.

The first one is our strong conditioning. I discuss this in more detail in my first book, *Reconditioning: Change your life in one minute* published in 2019.

Conditioning is what takes place in our sub-conscious mind from the time we are born. All we can do is act, talk and behave like the people around us. That is why we learnt the language we speak today. If there were two languages spoken in our home, we would speak two languages with no trouble. If there is one language spoken, we learn to speak that one, but when we grow older, we think: *Oh, I can't learn another language.* You can learn another language if you really want to. You can do anything, but strong conditioning has taken place to make you think, act and feel that you cannot achieve certain things and you never challenge that.

Usually we have very good ideas, but we do not take them to the next stage, or move towards our goals because of this strong conditioning. We are accustomed to fighting internal battles based on other people's perception of our abilities. We hear the negative voices whenever we want to do something groundbreaking. Those negative voices have a lot of power. Soon that power consumes us and we revert to what makes us comfortable—inaction.

The second barrier is outside of us. It is our environment.

We have a tendency to act like everybody around us. If you think about this, it does not make a lot of sense. If you study statistics, you will learn that 90.5 percent of people live their entire life not living the way they want to live, but responding to external pressure. They copy other people or are pressured to conform. In North America and Europe, rich continents in the world, people work productively for 40 years, out of their 65 working years, yet end up with hardly any money. There has to be something wrong. Only five percent end up comfortable or financially independent.

These statistics are not meant to depress anyone reading this book, but excite them at the possibility of being a disruptor or someone who thinks for themselves. When you get a job, you should not just have herd mentality and follow everybody else. You should ask yourself, *"Does everybody know what they are doing? Is there a better way to do it?"* This sets you apart from everyone else and makes you a better employee in the end.

Yet we are limited by our ideas. We do not want to be fired, so we take a number, stay in the line and wait for our turn. How boring and uneventful such life is. This attitude is great in the animal kingdom. Have you ever seen how ants behave? They are hard working and thrifty. These qualities have always seemed like good reasons for seeing ants as virtuous role models. Ants do the same thing repeatedly, year after year. They are knowledgeable and wise, but do not know enough to explore new ways of doing things. People, like ants, are chained by monotony and afraid to think beyond their conditioning. They cling onto certainties, doing things the same way every day. They live like ants.

Human beings are not supposed to live that way. We should make waves. We should stand out and be different, not for the sake of being different, but to make the world a better place and have some purpose in life. We have the capacity to do this because we think different thoughts from our family members, colleagues or peers. Finding your passion is not just about careers and money. It is about finding your authentic self. The one you have buried beneath other people's needs.

How do we do this? We should think and fill our minds with images of what we want to do and then set out to do it.

The Wright Brothers did that and they were the inventors of the aeroplane. Jeff Bezos did that and founded Amazon marketplace. Nelson Mandela did that and ended apartheid. Obama did that and became the first black president of the United States. There are many examples in the world.

These individuals are not different from us, but they stood out because they made a few waves. You do not have to go up to the Himalayas and become a guru. You can use what you have in your mind to change your worldview, your environment and yourself. You have to first imagine a different world and then move towards making it possible.

The best part of you that no one can ever see is not the physical, but the mental and intellectual capacity that you possess. This should be your starting point in knowing yourself. The physical body is nothing but the physical manifestation of the higher side of your personality. The body houses your mind and your intellect. It is simply a shell. What we have to study, in order to confront and deal with some of our challenges, is how our mind works. What happens when we think? Where do our thoughts come from? If we can build mental images in our minds, we are capable of building a physical replica of them in our world.

If I build an image of myself as a happy, relaxed person, I can live like that. If I build an image of me as prosperous, I can become prosperous. Similarly, if I build an image of myself as an unhappy, obnoxious, jealous and envious person, I become that too. Most gossipers depend on gossip for their happiness. They talk about other people and laugh at them. When they do not get a dose of gossip, they are lost.

When we know who we really are, we are already on the way to mending those family problems that we at first thought were difficult.

9. Victimhood

You have no control of your mind. You know that you were wrong and you blame other people for your failures because it makes you feel good to present yourself as a victim. This is the first stage in going down your downward slope.

Many times, we find excuses not to do something. We blame the other person—a friend, a family member, a parent, a partner or a colleague. It can be God, the devil, astrology or church. We think there is something out there that is doing something to us. People sometimes say from the stage, *'Why me?' 'Why is this happening to me again?' 'Why is my mother such a controlling freak?' 'Why am I unlucky in relationships?' 'It's not my fault, I wanted us to resolve this problem, but his family doesn't like me.'* That is the victim stage and victim mode.

When we do this, we exhibit lack of mind and soul control. We pass on our destiny to someone and we see problems and not opportunities. Interestingly, so many people live in that stage in their lives. Others live at this stage in parts of their lives. They could be a very successful executive at work, but having serious relationship problems with family members. Therefore, they are masterful at work, but a victim at home.

During this stage of victimhood, you are trying to forcefully make things happen and you want everyone, except yourself, to change. You do not know why you seem to help everyone, but nobody seems to help you. You get angry at people you help for not appreciating you, but you do not revel in the idea that you are helping them. You become a victim even when you are doing great things for others.

At this stage, you come up with big blame stories as to why your life is 'not working right'. You can be highly spiritually developed, rich, intelligent and sociable, but still fall into the victim stage. You could say, 'Why doesn't this person respond to my messages?' 'Why is my mother always asking me these questions; she is blocking my progress?' 'Why can't my sister or brother see the big contribution I have made to the family?'

Mark Manson writes in his book, *The Subtle Art of Not Giving a F*ck,* that when you get anxious about what others do to you, the anxiety makes you very unsettled and crippled. You start wondering why you are so anxious. So you become *anxious about being anxious*. You are now doubly anxious! Then you are anxious about your anxiety, and it causes you even more anxiety.

Take someone in the family, for example your sister, who has an anger problem. They get worried about something stupid, most inane stuff, and no one has an idea why. The fact that she is worried so easily starts to anger everyone in the family, and this angers her even more.

Then, in her rage, she realises that being angry all the time makes her a shallow and mean person, and she hates this. She hates it so much that she gets angry at herself and everyone else who is angry at her.

Everyone in the family then gets angry. But what are they angry about? No one remembers anymore, so no-one can solve a problem they do not know.

Manson calls this the 'Feedback Loop from Hell'. It causes problems in families. Those problems cause more problems and the loop continues like that until people stop talking to each other and spread gossip that complicates things even further. *Everyone is angry and about everyone being angry.*

So how do we break the Feedback Loop from Hell? We stop being victims. We examine ourselves, accept our limitations and strive to become the best we can by changing our thought process. We break the conditioning imposed on us by society, family and organisations.

This is not an easy process. It needs patience and constant practice. In the book *Reconditioning: Change your life in one minute*, I suggest taking baby steps and the power of incremental change. You cannot make bold steps to break conditioning that took many decades to be ingrained in you.

I use meditation to break conditioning and limiting thoughts and to break the Feedback Loop from Hell in my family. In meditation, they teach you about acceptance. I have had many meditation sessions where all they tell you is to 'accept and let it go'.

This is not the meditation that I am talking about. I am talking about that meditation where you really discover yourself. You lie on the bed and go deep into the life that you want and create the family that you would like to be part of.

You create that family in your mind and then you start working towards its creation. You meditate deeply on this until you start finding solutions to create harmony in your family. That which you desire deeply becomes your reality.

Another way is to write down your thoughts and views and use this journaling to break 'The Feedback Loop from Hell'. You have to start by accepting that there is a problem, and that you or the other person causes it. You have to ask yourself the following questions: 'What is the problem? Is it too bad to deal with? What are the ways to solve it?' Journaling is very helpful because writing about the problem makes you think about it, pay attention to it, and start to find solutions to it.

Lastly, you can use what is philosopher Alan Watts called the 'backwards law'.

Have you ever noticed that sometimes when you care less about something, you do better at it? Oftentimes, the person who is the least invested in the success of something is the one who actually ends up achieving it. Sometimes when you stop paying attention to something, everything seems to fall into place. This is all because of 'backwards law'.

What is interesting about the backwards law is that it is called "backwards" for a reason: not paying attention works in reverse. The failures in business are what lead to a better understanding of what is necessary to be successful. Being open with your insecurities paradoxically makes you more confident and charismatic around others.

The pain of honest confrontation is what generates the greatest trust and respect in your relationships. Suffering through your fears and anxieties is what allows you to build courage and perseverance.

Victimhood fights against the backwards law. It gives you silly excuses about not confronting your challenges. It causes friction in families and makes it difficult to move forward.

10. Visualisation

Have you ever caught yourself daydreaming to where it actually feels real? If so, keep doing it with some intention. Imagine in detail who you are spending time with, where you are living, travelling to, how much money you are making, and anything else you are trying to achieve. If you dream hard enough, you start seeing ideas that make those goals a reality.

Family problems arise from mental images that we create in our heads. These mental images or visualisations make unified family goals possible or impossible. Ask yourself this question: *Do we have a goal as a family or we are just a bunch of disjointed individuals competing with one another? Do I imagine a better family than the one I have today and am I doing something to make that possible?*

Families are organisations and just like any organisation, families need to have goals. Every member of this organisation must be able to contribute to the family's benefit, not compete to the family's detriment. When the family has unified goals in addition to each member's personal objectives, family relationships are stronger. Goals promote unity and cooperation and help each member to enjoy the fruits of the whole family's efforts.

A simple goal like, *'Let's spend time together'* can go a long way in resolving family feuds. Many family problems are caused by not knowing each another, because you do not spend time together. Family members can have hectic schedules and it may seem almost impossible to get everybody together at the same time. However, all members of the family must still make time to chat, eat dinner, or just sit down together.

These important moments should not be taken for granted as they bring about a multitude of benefits for a family. Spending quality time together can elevate a person's mood. It also provides the best opportunity to talk about important matters and to clarify any misunderstandings between family members.

Anything can qualify as family time and the simpler, the better. Family time allows its members to bond. It improves and strengthens familial relationships.

It is important to be specific about the family goal, to visualise how fun and exciting life will be after achieving that goal. In the book, *Think and Grow Rich,* Napoleon Hill teaches about setting goals. He says that, in order to achieve your goals, you have to describe, in specific terms, what you want to achieve and how great you will feel after achieving it.

It is not enough to say, 'I want to make a lot of money.' You have to be specific, for example, 'I want to make £5,000 in six months and buy a new car, by working a second job.' You can also say, 'I want to mend my relationship with my mother by calling her every day, working extra shifts so that I can save money to take her on a trip to Spain for Christmas.' These are real, achievable goals, not' 'I want to buy my mother a house.'

We are happy when thoughts become actions and when actions help us achieve goals. When thoughts come into your subconscious mind that you cannot do it, you have the ability to kick that thought out of your mind. Thinking about why you cannot do it, will not help you. Keep thinking, obsessively, that you can do it and soon you will find out how you can do it. The solutions 'will be shown' to you.

This is the power of visualisation.

If you take a look around, you will see nothing human-made that did not first exist as an image in someone's mind. It is impossible to create something that cannot be imagined first.

How would you do it?

Imagine the type of husband or wife that you want, obsess on it and soon you will start attracting only those sorts of people. In other words, being able to create someone in your head greatly increases your chances of being able to find that person in real life.

You may not realise this, but your brain is constantly using visualisation in the process of simulating future experiences, but this process happens so naturally that you generally are not even aware of it, the same way you usually are not aware that you are breathing.

If you are not aware of something, you are not actively directing the process. If you are not visualising a great family relationship, you are not actively participating in making it reality.

Many people fall in love with people they never imagined they would and when they have problems, they blame the person they fell in love with, not themselves.

This is wrong.

This is what creates future family problems, problems with parents, siblings, relatives and friends. You never gave thought to your decision to be with someone. You say, 'Oh I just found myself in love with them.' You were prepared to sacrifice your family for one person you never imagined being with in the first place.

You can learn to use visualisation to actively create future beautiful simulations that can help you improve the goals that you set for yourself. If you visualise the type of boyfriend you want, you can simulate how they will treat you, relate with your mother, your sister, your brother, your relatives and thus avoid potential family problems in the future. If you do this, you begin to exude energy and thoughts that attract such a person.

This is very important for your happiness. You simply cannot leave everything to chance. Life is too precious.

11. Mentor

You cannot simply leave your success to chance. Find someone who allows you to see the hope inside yourself and make them your mentor. This person will empower you to see a possible future, and believe that it can be obtained.

A ll of us are, at one point, like a blind man standing at the corner, waiting for somebody to lead us across," says former heavyweight boxer, Joe Frazier.

We need someone to reach out to who can help by throwing the lifeline to help us cross the treacherous waters that we could not navigate by ourselves. We grow from the people that can enrich our lives personally, professionally, spiritually and all the dimensions of our lives. We do not grow in a vacuum.

Find a mentor. Find someone who is already doing well in the area that you want to excel in and learn from them. It is pointless to go to your mother, father, sister, brother, relative or friend if they are not where you want to be, mentally and intellectually. Eventually you will run into problems with family members who do not understand your aspirations and your goals. Separate your family goals from individual goals, and do not expect your family members to understand your personal goals.

Just because someone is your family member, it does not mean that they should understand your goals or can be your mentor. It is pointless to go to a sick doctor if you want to get healed.

Mentors can help mould you into the person that you have always visualised yourself to be. If you want to be a great husband or wife, go to a person who is a great husband or wife. Learn from them. As painful as it sounds, your mother or sister may not be a great wife. Your brother may not be a great husband, so quit using them as mentors if that is your goal.

The great thing about a mentor is that he or she not only enhances your visualisation, but also shows you that it is possible to turn your visualisations into reality; that you are not simply building castles in the air. For example, if you really dream of doing something you have never tried before like having a happy, successful and supportive partner, you may have a difficult time simulating a detailed experience because you do not have much to draw on.

You will need to expose yourself to a mentor living that life. You may need to read books, watch videos, visit families, or talk to other people who have amazing family lives. Anything that increases your knowledge and awareness of what an experience would be like would help you to have more information to draw upon when creating your own visual simulation of a happy life.

You do not have to go to that person physically. You can grab that person's book–a great book–and study it like your life depends on it. I have been reading Napoleon Hill's *Think and Grow Rich* for 15 years. I will probably read it for the next ten. You too can choose your own book and obsess on it.

I have also been reading *The Power of Your Subconscious Mind* by Dr Joseph Murphy for over five years. It is one of the most powerful books you will ever find. You will learn about your mind, about conditioning and how it shapes your self-image, and it powers you to see yourself different from how you are today.

You may ask me, 'Why do you keep reading these books?'

There is value in reading and re-reading books; just like there is value in constantly talking to your mentor. The value is that I am always reminded of my conditioning and that I need to break it. I am human and I am fallible, so I need a constant reminder of my inadequacies, so that I can keep working on them. Authors of books are my mentors.

When you read a book that you have already read for the second time, you do not just see something new that you did not see before. You see something in yourself that you did not see before, or understand before. You grow. When you read, you create awareness. You break conditioning. You recondition. You get a free mentor.

So mentors give you the opportunity to create yourself, to discover something within yourself, and awaken and unleash your potential.

12. Attitude

A positive attitude is not just forcing a smile through gritted teeth in the hope of feeling better. It is something a lot more profound than that. When we adopt a positive attitude, we are using the power of our mind to remove thoughts and ideas that are no longer helping us to develop.

Attitude is an important aspect of our lives. In order to understand it well, it is important to realise that in life there are two states: the positive and negative states; the good and bad; the ying and the yang. Even the fifth immutable law of the universe – *The Law of Gender* – is clear that humans are made of feminine and masculine energies.

We have to train our mind to see the good in everything, the positive. If you fight with a family member, there is something to learn from it, but you may have to find what it is that you have to learn from that experience. You have to exercise your mind to do that. As the thought energy flows into our mind, we decide what we are going to think.

You can decide that your cousin is jealous of you or that she forgot to congratulate you on your success. You can decide to stop calling her, and she can be thinking that you are mad for some other reason. You can take a positive or negative attitude as the thought energy flows into your mind. If you take a positive attitude, you can start finding ways to deal with the issue.

You really have to understand how your conscious and your subconscious mind works in relation to your body or your physical world in order to understand attitude. Attitude should be taught as a subject in school ahead of reading, writing and math because it is a person's attitude that is going to determine the marks they get, the job they will get in future, and how they will avoid, or resolve, family problems.

Here is an example.

When I was young, my mother liked to make breakfast food at night as dinner every now and then. I remember one night in particular when she had made breakfast after a long, hard day at work.

On that evening so long ago, mother placed a plate of eggs, Vienna sausages and extremely burnt toast in front of my father. I remember waiting to see if anyone noticed! Yet, all my father did was reach for his toast, smile at my mother and ask me how my day was at school. I do not remember what I told him that night, but I remember watching him smear butter on that toast and enjoy every bite.

When I got up from the table that evening, I remember hearing my mother apologise
to my father for burning the bread. I will never forget what he said, "I love your cooking. You did well tonight."

Later that night, I went to say goodnight to my father and I asked him if he really enjoyed the burnt toast.

He said, "Your mum put in a hard day at work today and she's really tired. And besides, a little burnt toast never hurt anyone!"

My father had the right attitude. It helped avoid what could have been a family problem.

Life is full of imperfect things and imperfect people and the right attitude helps us create harmony amongst these imperfect people.

I am not the best at hardly anything, and I forget birthdays and anniversaries just like everyone else, but what I have learnt over the years is that learning to accept each other's faults—and choosing to celebrate each other's differences—is one of the most important keys to creating a healthy, growing, and lasting relationship and a happy family. Our attitude helps us celebrate those differences, not question them.

That's my prayer for you for life. Change your attitude and learn to take the good, the bad and the ugly parts of other people's lives and your life and acknowledge them. A burnt piece of bread was not a deal-breaker for my father because he had a positive attitude to life!

We could extend this to any relationship. In fact, attitude is the base of any relationship, be it a husband-wife or parent-child or friend-friend relationship!

Don't put the key to your happiness in someone else's pocket. Create your happiness with your positive attitude.

13. Self-image

There are lot of people with loads of money, but have poverty of the mind and soul. Money will only give you options, but it will never bring happiness to a poor mind and poor soul.

In the last pages, I talked about goal setting and attitude to solve family and other problems. In this chapter, I discuss the issue of image, especially self-image. When we think, we build images in our minds.

Dr Maxwell Maltz wrote extensively on the issue of self-image in the 1960s. He was a plastic surgeon who founded the study called Cybernetics, a word loosely translated from Greek and meaning *to steer a ship to port.*

Psycho-Cybernetics is a term coined by Dr. Maltz, which means, "steering your mind to a productive, useful goal so you can reach the greatest port in the world, peace of mind."

He realised, during his surgeries that whenever he removed a scar from a patient or if they had a nose job, there was a great psychological change in that person. They may have been introverted, lonely and staying by themselves, and suddenly they became social, gregarious and outgoing.

Dr Maltz postulated that there must be two images that we have: an exterior or outside image and also an inner self-image. This prompted him to write a book called *Psycho-Cybernetics*; psycho being the mind and cybernetics being the cycle of control and communication. He explains how every one of us has an image in our mind of our self (called a self-image). That image can either help us progress towards our goal or limit us and stop us from achieving our goal.

Too many people do not know much about themselves, so they do not have a very good image of themselves. You will often notice people not directly looking at you, are shy, look up and down and avoid talking to you. They will never try to do anything of any great consequence because they do not think they can. They have a poor self-image.

Part of the reason why we have a poor self-image is that in school we are taught or *conditioned* that we do not do well in certain subjects, and in others. So, when we come across that which we were told we couldn't do well, we fail. A great example is the IQ test. Alfred Binet, the Frenchman who developed the IQ test, branded people good, bad, smart, not smart. That is not true. We can change our IQ by changing our self-image.

If we are conditioned by being constantly told that we are like our dads or mums, that we can never succeed in arithmetic because we are good in the arts, that becomes our thought process, our truth, our self-image, our *conditioning*. That is all false. We should be encouraging a child by giving them a pat on the back, rather than a kick.

We all have self-image and, no matter how good you think your self-image is, you can improve it. You can do this by visualising, fantasising or dreaming about how you want to live your life, and then start thinking of ways you will make that possible.

That is a picture in your mind.

When you pick up a book, that book is nothing but a picture that an author has *painted in words*. Vincent van Gogh was asked how he paints such beautiful pictures. He said, *'I dream my painting and then I paint my dream'*.

If we relax and build a picture in our mind, about how we want to see ourselves, we can create beautiful self-images. We can create beautiful family images; images of love; images of great family lives; images of harmony and peace.

The following story is about my two friends who also happen to be my favourite couple, Tina and Harold. They love books and they spend many hours in bookshops, new and second-hand, prowling for good reads. They consider these moments as precious family times.

Harold works in the British army and often the couple manipulates the 'military system' as much as they can, trying to prevent a long, dreaded absence from one another.

One day, they were, delaying the inevitable, passing time in a second hand bookstore, with their children. They were as broke as they had ever been, yet they were grateful to be together. They seized every opportunity for extra hugs, shared daydreams and laughter.

There was only one other person in the bookstore, besides the proprietor, a lovely, well-dressed woman, about Tina's age. Tina noticed her clothes, her shoes and her expensive handbag, and wondered what it would be like to be rich enough to walk into a bookstore and have the money to buy any book her heart desired. However, they were having so much fun, that she quickly forgot about the woman.

They joked as they continued their treasure hunt, clutching their spending money of ten pounds each, each hoping to be the first to find the oldest, least expensive book. It was a bittersweet excursion. Frequently Tina and Harold would brush past one another, finding excuses to touch or to give another's hand an extra squeeze.

Tina remembered that there was an ATM machine, not far from the bookstore, and she decided that she needed another twenty pounds that she had squirreled away.

"Not fair!" Louise, her eldest daughter, cried, laughing. "The rest of us can only spend ten pounds, and here you're going to have thirty pounds!"

They all laughed, and began to tease Tina, mercilessly, but she was able to convince them that she must have the thirty pounds, in order to get that irresistible book.

"Come on, Tina," Harold laughed. "I'll drive you to the ATM."

Then they did another round of hugging and kissing, none of them wanting to be apart for even a few minutes.

Soon they would be saying goodbye. They could not resist the opportunity to assure one another of their love, and their faith that their separation would soon end. It must have been a curious ballet, this demonstrative family scene, but they were oblivious to what others might think.

Military families seem to fall into two categories: those who look for affectionate opportunities, and those who avoid close contact, because goodbyes are painful. They have different attitudes to life.

Their family was a 'huggy-kissy' family. Not mindful of anyone else, they continued to give kisses and hugs all around. In Harold's military career, they had become painfully aware that anything could happen during even the briefest separation.

Finally, in between another hug and kiss, they saw the perfect book for Harold! It was one hundred years old, and it was on his favourite period–the Middle Ages. Tina quickly checked the inside cover for the price, and her heart fell. It was seventy-five pounds. They did not have it. She looked up at Harold, already knowing the answer.

He really wanted that book. Tina could see the pain in his eyes. She reached out and gave him an extra hug. He understood her 'honey, we just can't afford it' message. She leaned into his sheltering arms, and saw that the well-dressed woman was also touching the book that she wanted.

'Ah well, let her have it,' she said to herself.

Tina gave Harold and extra hug, and half-serious, she murmured, as her eyes locked with his.

"Oooohh, I wish I were rich!"

"It looks to me, as though you already are!" The rich woman standing next to them said with a smile.

A pause stretched through eternity and Tina's heart filled with comprehension. She looked up at her husband, and gazed at her daughters, wrapped as they were in the arms of love, and she knew it. She was rich, very rich. She quickly turned to thank the woman for her gentle reminder, but she was gone!

Who was she? She will never know. However, what she did for her outlook was nothing short of miraculous. Tina said she would never forget her.

Where did she disappear to? She could not say.

Strangely enough, within days, Harold received a job offer in London. In less than two weeks, he was hired and they moved to the place that is now their home in Hammersmith. The job notice had been sent out two days before the incident at the bookshop, even as they hugged and kissed and wished in that bookshop.

Even as they heard the words, "It looks to me, as though you already are," events were already in motion to unite their family.

Tina was quite certain that it was all part of a divine plan, to remind her of what being rich was all about—faith, love, family and friends. It was also about self-image. She did not see herself as rich as she was concerned about money all time.

Country singer Dolly Parton once said, "You can be rich in spirit, kindness, love and all those things that you can't put a dollar sign on."

The impotence of money is felt when one is so ill that they face death in the face. We have learnt this important lesson during this very trying period of Coronavirus pandemic. All the riches in the world will not offer you the comfort that you need when the inevitability of death hits you in the face.

You need family and friends. So while you break your family further by not putting in time for them, by working to get rich, always remember that 'you are already rich' and should change your self-image.

The one point that all the self-improvement teachers agree about throughout history and have been unanimous about, is that *we become what we think about.* It makes a lot of sense. It may sound like fantasy at first. It might even appear to be a lie, but if you read it often enough, you start to believe it.

When William James said, 'Believe in your belief and you create the fact" you see people's personality begin to change.

Our thoughts control our feelings, and our feelings control our actions. We hear gossip about how bad our family member is. We get upset and stop talking to that family member. We create our own doom and gloom and we respond to it.

When an idea comes into my mind from someone, I reason with it. I do not just swallow it hook, line and sinker. I question, *'Will it help me get to a better place with a family member?'* If it doesn't, I reject the idea.

14. Building bridges

If you cannot forgive others, you break the bridge over which you must pass yourself. Make sure you are always building bridges and not walls because those walls may be blocking your progress.

I attended a business development seminar back in 2000. One of the trainers–a very smart man from Singapore–told us a story about helping people strengthen their family ties. It was a very inspiring story and I still remember it vividly.

The story is about two brothers who lived on adjoining farms. One day they fell into conflict. It was the first serious rift in 40 years of farming side-by-side, sharing machinery, and trading labour and goods as needed, without a hitch. Then the long collaboration fell apart.

It began with a small misunderstanding and it grew into a major difference. Finally, it exploded into an exchange of bitter words, followed by weeks of silence.

One morning, there was a knock on John's door. He opened it to find a man with a carpenter's toolbox.

"I'm looking for a few days work," he said. "Perhaps you would have a few small jobs here and there I could help with? Could I help you?"

"Yes," said the older brother. "I do have a job for you. Look across the creek at that farm. That's my neighbour. In fact, it's my younger brother! Last week, there was a meadow between us. He recently took his bulldozer to the river levee, and now there is a creek between us. Well, he may have done this to spite me, but I'll do him one better.

"See that pile of lumber by the barn? I want you to build me a fence – an 8-foot fence – so I won't need to see his place, or his face, anymore."

The carpenter said, "I think I understand the situation. Show me the nails, and the post-hole digger, and I'll be able to do a job that pleases you."

The older brother had to go to town, so he helped the carpenter get the
materials ready and then he was off for the day.

The carpenter worked hard all that day – measuring, sawing, and nailing. About sunset, when the farmer returned, the carpenter had just finished his job.

The farmer's eyes opened wide and his jaw dropped. There was no fence there at all. It was a bridge. It stretched from one side of the creek to the other. It was a fine piece of work, with handrails and all!

The neighbour, his younger brother, was coming toward them, his hand outstretched.

He said, "You are quite a guy to build this bridge, after all I've said and done to you. I am amazed at your capacity to mend things, especially our broken family relationships."

The two brothers stood at each end of the bridge and then they met in the middle, taking each other's hand. They turned to see the carpenter hoist his toolbox onto his shoulder.

"No, wait! Stay a few days. I've a lot of other projects for you," said the older brother.

"I'd love to stay on," the carpenter said, "but I have many more bridges to build."

Pride is a disease. It builds walls, not bridges and it destroys family ties and important relationships. Throughout my life, I have many examples of people building walls by their pride, their attitude, but very few examples of people building bridges.

I live in the hope that people will draw together, if not physically, then at least emotionally. This is essential for the peace that we all strive for. Building bridges is not an easy process. It takes time and effort, but once the bridge is built, it is strong, stable and even looks beautiful.

One way we can all build bridges is to put effort in the way we connect and communicate. You start by looking at your own faults, not the other person's. Then change and start building bridges that mend our broken families.

The wise always build bridges in times of crisis, the foolish dig in and double down on building walls.

15. Age differences, imprints and conditioning

Existential philosopher Albert Camus said: *"You will never be happy if you continue to search for what happiness consists of. You will never live if you are looking constantly for the meaning of life."*

When we are born, we are imprinted with everything that is happening in our lives. We have imprints from our family, our society and these imprints condition us to become something other than ourselves.

We have emotional contagion from our parents whose relationships were not working at the time we were born, and from what is going on in our world. We learn how to adapt, how to adjust, and how to survive throughout our lives.

Sometimes a crisis happens in our lives. The crisis makes us see that we have been living a life that is too small. We realise that we have been living a life that is conditioned by our families. For example, you fall in love with someone older, or someone who is not from your country or your race, and society has an issue with that. You become a single parent and society has an issue with that.

You choose your own career and your family has an issue with that. This causes problems and friction because you are breaking the conditioning. You are destroying the imprint that should guide your life. You are breaking free from what is expected of you, to do what is best for you.

Nothing can stop us from reaching our destiny. We have to understand our mind and our soul to realise that there is no problem, only possibilities. The story of Monica, who was older than her boyfriend demonstrates how understanding your mind and your purpose can overcome even the most difficult family problems.

Monica looked no more than 30 and her grooming was impeccable. Only her hands and a few telltale wrinkles on her neck revealed that she was closing in on 50. Tendai was 25, loved Monica's wit, generosity, and great looks. The 25-year age difference did not matter to either of them, but it mattered a whole lot to Tendai's parents. They were furious that Tendai had selected Monica.

"She's too old to have children," they wailed.

"When you're in your prime, she'll be an old lady," they moaned.

"You could have anyone you wanted; why would you marry someone old enough to be your mother?" They screamed.

A number of issues soured the in-law relationship. It is not uncommon for mothers-in-law to feel threatened when their daughters-in-law are older than their sons. In their minds, the role of the mother is replaced. In these situations, the competitiveness that accompanies most mother-in-law/daughter-in-law relationships is usually intensified.

A mother may feel uncomfortable to realise that her son is in a relationship with a woman closer to her own age. This is apt to intensify if she no longer feels attractive. A mother-in-law might also worry that an older woman has seduced her young boy. Commonly in these situations, a mother- and father-in-law worry that they will never have grandchildren, because their daughter-in-law is over the hill.

There is usually not such a flap when an older man marries a younger woman.

In this instance, it is important to pay attention to family concerns, but ultimately, it is also about mind shift. Problems like these can create the Feedback Loop from Hell discussed elsewhere in this book. You get anxious about how, as an older woman, you are not accepted by the family of your younger husband. Then you get more anxious because of your anxiety and that shows to everyone who meets you and they get anxious because of your anxiety.

Yet this is part of the beauty of being human. Very few animals on earth have the ability to think cogent thoughts to begin with, but we humans have the luxury of being able to have thoughts *about* our thoughts. This is the miracle of consciousness and we should embrace it so that we can start finding solutions in response.

One of the solutions is to take charge. Do not wait for the in-laws to come to you. Discuss the issue of the parents with your spouse first. Sometimes, there are many age issues to work out between the couple too, so that is where everything should start. Get your significant other involved because you cannot fight this battle alone.

It is important to present a unified front. It will not work if he sits there and says, "Yeah, well my parents have a point. You are old!" He should simply tell your in-laws that they do not have to love you, but they must respect you. As your in-laws see your relationship last, they will move from respect to like and maybe even to love.

The bottom line is to demand respect.

Statistically, marriages are most likely to succeed when the partners share common interests–but there are no carved-in-granite rules about ideal age differences between spouses. However, if you and your spouse are comfortable with each other's ages, then it will at least give you some solid ground with which to deal with any nay-saying in-laws.

It is important to realise that **demanding respect needs a mind shift. It requires that one break from the imprint and conditioning that society imposes on couples with big age differences.** For most people seeking a break, the conditioning has become a borderline epidemic, making them overly stressed, overly neurotic, and overly self-loathing because.

They feel bad about feeling bad. They feel guilty for feeling guilty. They get angry about getting angry. They get anxious about feeling anxious. This leads to serious family problems with no solution in sight.

A mind shift helps the older woman to stop hating herself for feeling so bad after loving a younger man. Older men who fall in love with younger women do not feel bad, but only because society has accepted their type of relationship. There is no other reason. It is a result of conditioning, of imprinting.

Lastly, one can use what was referred to above as "backwards law" to deal with problems with in-laws and age differences. The idea is not to keep trying to feel better about your relationship, but to shift your mind.

The more you pursue feeling better all the time, the less satisfied you become. This is like pursuing something relentlessly. It only reinforces the fact that you lack it in the first place. The more you desperately want to be rich, the more poor and unworthy you feel, regardless of how much money you actually make.

The more you desperately want to be sexy and desired, the uglier you come to see yourself, regardless of your actual physical appearance.

The more you desperately want to be happy and loved, the lonelier and more afraid you become, regardless of those who surround you.

The more you want to be spiritually enlightened, the more self-centered and shallow you become in trying to get there.

16. Parent-child bliss

In the happiest of our childhood memories, our parents were happy, too.

My friend, John, told me a story about his relationship with his mother. After 10 years of marriage, his wife wanted him to take another woman out to dinner and a movie.

The wife said to him, "I love you, but I know this other woman loves you too, and she would love to spend some time with you."

The other woman that his wife wanted him to visit was his mother, who had been a widow for 19 years, but the demands of his work and his three children had made it possible to visit her only occasionally. That night he called to invite his mother to go out for dinner and a movie.

"What's wrong, are you well?" she asked him.

His mother was the type of woman who suspected that a late night call or a surprise invitation was a sign of bad news.

"I thought that it would be pleasant to spend some time with you," he responded. "Just the two of us."

She thought about it for a moment, and then said, "I would like that very much."

That Friday after work, as he drove over to pick her up, he was a bit nervous. When he arrived at her house, he noticed that she, too, seemed to be nervous about their date. She waited in the door with her coat on. She had a new haircut and was wearing the dress that she had worn to celebrate her last wedding anniversary. She smiled from a face that was as radiant as an angel's.

"I told my friends that I was going to go out with my son, and they were impressed," she said, as she got into the car.

"They can't wait to hear about our meeting."

They went to a restaurant that, although not elegant, was very nice and cosy. John's mother took his arm as if she were the First Lady. After they sat down, he had to read the menu. Her eyes could only read large print. Half way through the entries, he lifted his eyes and saw his mother sitting there staring at him. A nostalgic smile was on her lips.

"It was I who used to have to read the menu when you were very young," she said.

"Then it's time that you relax and let me return the favour," John responded.

During the dinner, they had an agreeable conversation – nothing extraordinary, but catching up on recent events of each other's life. They talked so much that they missed the movie.

As they arrived at her house later, she said, "I'll go out with you again, but only if you let me invite you." John agreed.

"How was your dinner date?" asked John's wife when he got home.

"Very nice. Much more so than I could have imagined," he answered.

A few days later, John's mother died of a massive heart attack. It happened so suddenly that he did not have a chance to do anything for her. Sometime later, he received an envelope with a copy of a restaurant receipt from the same place they had dined. An attached note said: "I paid this bill in advance. I wasn't sure that I could be there, but I paid for two plates – one for you and the other for your wife. You will never know what that night meant for me. I love you, son."

At that moment, John understood the importance of saying, in time, "I love you."

He also understood the importance of giving loved ones the time they deserve. Nothing is more important in life than family. Family should not be put off until *some other time*.

The best present you can give a parent is a few minutes of your time each day. It is a tragedy that, in some families, so much is asked of parents, and so little is given.

Do not be so busy growing up, that you forget that your parents are also growing old and need your support.

The only truly selfless love is parental love. It is unconditional and forgiving. Yet the irony is that we will only know the love of a parent when we become parents ourselves.

The love of a parent is the only love that is continuous and that goes beyond heartbreak and disappointment. No one, except your parent, is obligated to love you. From everyone else, you have to earn it. You have to work for it. It does not come free.

17. Never give up

George Bernard Shaw wrote: "A happy family is but an earlier heaven."

The following story is about family love and was reported in a US women's magazine some years back.

Like any good mother, when Karen found out that another baby was on the way, she did what she could to help her 3-year-old son, Michael, prepare for a new sibling. They found out that the new baby was going be a girl, and day after day, night after night, Michael sang to his s sister in mummy's tummy. He was building a bond of love with his little sister before he even met her.

The pregnancy progressed normally for Karen, an active member of the Creek United Methodist Church in Morristown, Tennessee in the United States of America. In time, the labour pains came. Soon it was every five minutes, every three, every minute, but serious complications arose during delivery and Karen found herself in hours of labour. *Would a C-section be required?*

Finally, after a long struggle, Michael's little sister was born, but she was in very serious condition. With a siren howling in the night, the ambulance rushed the infant to the neonatal intensive care unit at St. Mary's Hospital, Knoxville, Tennessee.

The days inched by. The little girl got worse. The paediatrician had to tell the parents there was very little hope.

"Be prepared for the worst," she said. Karen and her husband contacted a local cemetery about a burial plot. They had fixed up a special room in their house for their new baby, but they found themselves having to plan for a funeral. Michael, however, kept begging his parents to let him see his sister.

"I want to sing to her," he kept saying.

Week two in intensive care looked as if a funeral would come before the week was over. Michael kept nagging about singing to his sister, but kids are not allowed in intensive care. Karen decided to take Michael whether they liked it or not. If he did not see his sister right then, he may never see her alive.

She dressed him in an oversized scrub suit and marched him into ICU. He looked like a walking laundry basket. The head nurse recognised him as a child and bellowed, "Get that kid out of here now. No children are allowed."

The mother rose up strong in Karen, and the usually mild-mannered woman glared steel-eyed right into the head nurse's face, her lips a firm line.

"He is not leaving until he sings to his sister," she stated.

Then Karen towed Michael to his sister's bedside. He gazed at the tiny infant losing the battle to live. After a moment, he began tossing.

In the pure-hearted voice of a 3-year-old, Michael sang: *You are my sunshine, my only sunshine; you make me happy when skies are grey.*

Instantly, the baby girl seemed to respond. The pulse rate began to calm down and become steady.

"Keep on singing, Michael," encouraged Karen with tears in her eyes. "You never know, dear, how much I love you, please don't take my sunshine away."

As Michael sang to his sister, the baby's ragged, strained breathing became as smooth as a kitten's purr.

"Keep on singing, sweetheart."

The other night, dear, as I lay sleeping, I dreamed I held you in my arms, he sang.

Michael's little sister began to relax as rest, healing rest, seemed to sweep over her.

"Keep singing, Michael."

Tears had now conquered the face of the bossy head nurse. Karen glowed.

You are my sunshine, my only sunshine. Please don't take my sunshine away...

The next, day, the very next day, the little girl was well enough to go home.

Woman's Day Magazine called it 'The Miracle of a Brother's Song'. The medical staff just called it a miracle.

This story is about family love and the strong bond of family. Never forget who was with you from the start.

Michael had a strong bond with his sister well before she was born. That bond was strong enough to save her life.

The family unit is the first organisation that you are a part of. While there are obvious exceptions, there is usually an intrinsic trust built into your family. You may later experience problems and challenges, but always remember the protection and love that you got when you were vulnerable and needed it the most.

On the outside, it may look like you have fallen apart, but as a family, you always stay together in your hearts, bonded together for life, no matter where you rest your head.

Family may be defined as a group of people who are related to each other, but it is more than that. It is a meaningful connection, an *experience*. It is an incredible and unbreakable bond—created by mothers, fathers, sisters, brothers.

It is comfort in a world of uncertainty. It is a shoulder to lean on. It is a source of inspiration. It is love and support. It is that warm and fuzzy feeling. It is wonderful, and it is necessary.

Irish playwright, critic, polemicist and political activist, George Bernard Shaw, wrote: "A happy family is but an earlier heaven." George Santayana called family 'one of nature's masterpieces'. I have found family to be the compass that guides me all the time.

I may wander with friends and acquaintances, but I always come back to family when push comes to shove. I find it as the ultimate inspiration to reach great heights.

Family has always provided the comfort that I need whenever I falter. It is the only rock that I know that has stayed steady in my life, in spite of

the difficulties that I sometimes face with family members.

18. Take action

The real measure of intelligence is action. Don't wait because the time will never really be right. If you don't start, you have already failed before you begin.

Too many people put off something that brings them joy and brings them closer to their family members just because they have not thought about it. They do not have it on their schedule. The excuse is that they did not know it was coming or are too rigid to depart from their routine.

I recently read a book about the victims of the 9/11 bombings in New York in 2001. Many of them talked about missed opportunities with their loved ones who perished at the World Trade Centre.

One woman in particular said she had missed many opportunities to spend time with her deceased husband because she was too busy with work. She was always putting off their dinner dates.

That fateful morning on September 11, she put off a breakfast date that would have saved her husband.

The husband went to work instead, and 30 minutes later, terrorists attacked the World Trade Centre and he died.

How often do you drop in to talk to your parent(s) and you sit in silence while you watch a film on television or click on your smartphone?

I cannot count the times I called my brother and said, "How about going to lunch in a half hour?" He would gas up and stammer, "I can't. I have to get home early and work on a project. I wish I had known yesterday, I had a late breakfast, it looks like it's going to rain." My personal favorite is: "It's Monday."

He died a few years ago. We never had that lunch together.

We cram so much into our lives and we tend to schedule our headaches into our lives. We live on a sparse diet of promises we make to ourselves when all the conditions are perfect!

Some of our excuses are:

I will go back and visit my mother when I get some money.

We will invite visitors and entertain when we replace the living-room carpet.

We will go on holiday after we get a new car.

Life has a way of accelerating, as we get older. The days get shorter and the list of promises to ourselves gets longer. One morning we awaken and all we have to show for our lives is a litany of *I am going to, I plan on*, and *someday, when things are settled down a bit.*

I have a 'seize the moment' sister-in-law. She is open to adventure and available for trips. She keeps an open mind on new ideas. Her enthusiasm for life is contagious. You talk with her for five minutes, and you are ready to go on a zip line in Morocco or scuba diving in Turkey.

I had not bought myself a new pair of sunglasses in five years. I love sunglasses. The other day, I stopped the car and bought myself two designer ones. If my car had hit a pole on the way home, I would have died happy.

Now... go on and have a nice day. Do something you *want* to do, not something on your 'should do' list. If you were going to die soon and had only one phone call you could make, who would you call and what would you say? Why are you waiting?

When the day is done, do you lie in your bed with the next hundred chores running through your head? Have you ever told your child, your mother, your friend, your relative, "We'll do it tomorrow"?

In your haste, do you not see their sorrow? Have you lost touch and your soul along the way? Have you ever let a good friendship die? Have you ever called just to say "Hi"?

When you worry and hurry through your day, it is like an unopened gift thrown away. Life is not a race. Take it slower. Hear the music before the song is over. Mend relationships before it is too late.

19. A mother's sacrifice

You will not be in your children's memories tomorrow if you are not in their lives today. I owe everything that I am to my mother, all my success in life is because of the intellectual, moral, and physical education I received from her.

This chapter was inspired by a story of one of my late friends who died before she had made amends with her mother. They always fought and spent many years not talking to each other.

I know they were both hurting because I tried many times to bring them together, but failed. My friend was set in her ways. She thought her mother had disrespected her—whatever that meant. I always said to her my mother could never disrespect me. She can tell me things I do not want to hear, but I always think that those comments come from a place of love.

Some mother do indeed hurt and hate their children, but they are rare.

Nyarai died before her mother and she was very devastated by the death. I met her many years after her daughter's death and she was suffering from mental health problems – talking to herself and her imaginary daughter all the time. I felt the pain and agony that she was going through. Parents never think they will outlive their children.

I know this well because my brother was the first one to die in our family and my father never came to terms with it. He cut a lonely figure, in constant pain, in the immediate period after my brother's death.

He would say to me, "Son, I have to go and see where your brother is. He is my son and every day I live on this earth, I am abandoning him."

He only managed a couple of years before he followed my brother to Heaven. I am sure they are now both at peace.

Nyarai's mother is not at peace. Please mend your relationships before it is too late.

When I thought about expressing my love towards my mother, my fingers started tripping with lots of enthusiasm while I typed. With the numberless thoughts in my mind, I was confused a little. Which words would I use? Her selfless and unconditional love which I cannot experience anywhere on this planet, made it difficult for me to pick the right words and moments.

....

She dreamed of me from the time she was a little girl cradling a baby doll in her arms in Highfields township in Zimbabwe. She always saw me playing around the little yard at her family home there in Highfields in her childhood dreams.

She carried me in her body and I made her sick every morning for weeks and weeks. She bore me into the world through intense pain, but when she heard me cry and saw my wrinkled face, she forgot all about it and wept tears of joy.

She fed me at her breast and her whole world revolved around me.

She stole into my room at night just to watch me sleep and she was sure I was the most beautiful child on earth. She set up through the night to bathe away the fever and at breakfast my father said, "Did you sleep well, son?" oblivious to the all-night vigil held by my mother.

She somehow always knew when I needed her, even in the middle of the night, and she came to my room, changed my bedding, and made sure I was warm and dry.

She covered my ears, gave me my coat, and checked my homework. She made me practice reading to become one of the best pupils in my class. She nagged me to brush my teeth with words of wisdom like, "Be true to your teeth or they will be false to you."

She changed my nappies and cleaned up when I was sick and washed underwear no one else would touch without a chemical suit. The cakes she baked made me forget the beating I took from the neighborhood bully or the canning I got from the teachers.

She listened to me and did not laugh when others would mock me. She believed in me when I did not believe in myself and prayed for me even when I did not think I needed it. She made me think I could do things I was sure I could not do. She was tough enough to call my bluff, discipline me, and give me a sense of boundaries and the security that comes with it.

She knew when I needed a spanking or just a nap and she did not always give me sweets though she longed to indulge me.

She was always waiting when I came in late. When I complained about it, she pretended to be asleep the way I always did when I wanted her to carry me to bed when I dosed off on the sofa watching television.

She read the Bible to me, read the Bible in front of me and did what mothers had to do to make sure the family was faithful in church. She made my dad a much better man than he ever would have been without her.

She mended clothes as a labour of love and it broke her heart to see how quickly I grew out of them. She knew I was only loaned to her from God and soon the house would fall silent again. She washed mountains of dishes and truckloads of laundry. She put up food on the hottest summer days and did not complain.

Her most sincere prayers were the ones she sent heavenward in gratitude for all of us, her children. She filled our home with fragrance and beauty and music – the smell of fresh-cut flowers and *fat cooks* for breakfast and Sunday lunch. Her eyes were bright, happy, and full of life. She wept though, wept and worried a thousand times for us when no one ever knew.

She rose early during school holidays when all my cousins, nieces and nephews were at our house so we could enjoy a festive meal and an enduring memory. She planned for days and worked for hours so that in a few minutes we could gulp it down and go and play outside. We did not always thank her or help her, but those meals have been a cherished memory for years.

She baked us special treats just to watch us eat them. Something inside made her happier the more we ate.

She wore old dresses so we could have school uniforms. She never went on holiday so we could go on school trips and Scout camps. She never had hobbies so she could afford school fees. She was happy with old time fashion so we could have tennis shoes. She did not abandon the family when our father was insensitive to her needs. She took the blame for our failures, stood back, and let our father have the glory for our successes.

In addition, having done all these things and a thousand others that make *mother* a sacred word, she still felt that she was not the mother she should have been.

20. Priorities

Family time is not a matter of convenience; it is a matter of priority. Spend time with those you love because one of these days you will say one of the following two statements: "I wish I had" or "I'm glad I did".

I grew up in Harare and had a friend called Tinashe. His father, Nhamo, was a great man who wanted his family to succeed and he did everything he could to make sure that his family lived a great life.

Nhamo was a hardworking man who delivered bread for a living, in order to support his wife and three children, including my friend Tinashe. He spent all his evenings after work attending classes, hoping to improve himself so that he could one day find a better paying job. Except for Sundays, Nhamo hardly ate a meal together with his family. He worked and studied very hard because he wanted to provide his family with the best money could buy.

Whenever the family complained that he was not spending enough time with them, he reasoned that he was doing all this for them, but he often yearned to spend more time with his family.

The day came when the examination results were announced. To his joy, Nhamo passed with distinctions. Soon after, he was offered a good job as a senior supervisor. The job paid handsomely.

Like a dream come true, Nhamo could now afford to provide his family with life's little luxuries like nice clothing, fine food and holidays in South Africa and other places. However, the family still did not get to see Nhamo for most of the week. He continued to work very hard, hoping to be promoted to the position of manager. In fact, to make himself a worthy candidate for the promotion, he enrolled for another course with the newly opened Zimbabwe Open University.

Again, whenever the family complained that he was not spending enough time with them, he reasoned that he was doing all this for them, but he often yearned to spend more time with his family.

Nhamo's hard work paid off and he was promoted. Jubilantly, he decided to hire a maid to relieve his wife from her domestic tasks. He also felt that their three-room house was no longer big enough and it would be nice for his family to be able to enjoy the facilities and comfort of a much larger suburban house.

Having experienced the rewards of his hard work many times before, Nhamo resolved to further his studies and work at being promoted again. The family still did not get to see much of him. In fact, sometimes Nhamo had to work on Sundays entertaining clients.

Again, whenever the family complained that he was not spending enough time with them, he reasoned that he was doing all this for them, but he often yearned to spend more time with his family.

As expected, Nhamo's hard work paid off again and he bought a beautiful house in Borrowdale – one of the finest places in Harare, Zimbabwe. On the first Sunday evening at their new home, Nhamo declared to his family that he decided not to take any more courses or pursue any more promotions. From then on, he was going to devote more time to his family.

Nhamo did not wake up the next day.

You determine what is important to you by the amount of time you dedicate to it *now*. No amount of success or money can replace the amount of time spent with family.

Willie Williams, the author of the parenting book, *7 Steps to Parenting Power* observes, "If I could attribute any one thing to the success my family has experienced through the years, it would simply be my wife and I took the time to be there for our kids."

It is important to remember that there is no success that can ever compensate for failure in the home. You fail at home; you fail everywhere and vice versa.

According to the late philanthropist Mother Teresa, "If you want to change the world, go home and love your family."

If there is a great lesson I have learnt thus far in my life, it is that spending time with my family does not mean I have lost your ambition. I strive for my family, I define success for myself.

Success, for me, is measured by the amount of happiness in my family and the smiles on my wife and children's faces. It is not measured by the amount of money I have in my bank account.

21. Hotel rooms

We may wander everywhere and enjoy many things. Most of these are ephemeral. The only rock that stays put, that stays steady, the only institution that really works in the end, is the family.

Every time I step into my hotel room, I get excited. On one particular day, I stepped into a big room, surrounded by an inviting king-size bed, flanked by overstuffed armchairs that rested against sliding glass doors that opened onto a private patio. A small dining table sat next to a kitchenette with a separate sink, refrigerator and coffee machine.

"Wow," I thought to myself. "Nice place."

I love hotels – from the Holiday Inn Express to the Ritz-Carlton and everything in between. I love to enter a clean room, hang my clothes and gaze out the window, walk out in the morning knowing that each afternoon when I return, someone else will have made the bed. I like in-room dining and the way they greet you so professionally: "Nice to have you with us again, Mr. Garande."

The problem is that unless my family travels with me, I never sleep well in these great hotels. I toss, turn, and worry about my children and my wife. Even though my children find a way to interrupt even the best night's sleep at home, still, I would rather be with them. I will take my son Sean clamouring over me at seven in the morning or my daughter, Maya's singing over the finest linens and a chocolate on my pillow. When I am on the road, I yearn for my loved ones.

I am deeply troubled by the number of parents who realise too late that their children grew up too fast. In the hustle-bustle of career and corporate rat race, they missed their childhood.

What they fail to say, but too often inwardly think causes me even more pain: "I barely even know them."

This applies to couples as well. They are so in a hurry to get who-knows-where – a destination seldom defined. Relationships turn into co-habitations, romance into convenience. This is very disturbing.

A hundred years from now, no one will remember the size of your bank account, the car you drove or the square footage of your house. The world might differ greatly based on your impact in the life of a small child. Your life will most certainly improve, if you pay attention to your significant others. Make the choice to them first. Your example will benefit the rest of us. Our world cries out for role models and heroes of everyday living.

What could you do today to let your loved ones know how much they mean to you? What will you do tomorrow and the next day?

Think of one specific action that you can take, and take it. Then think of another one and take that, too. Challenge yourself to find new ways to express your appreciation and love on a daily basis. It will pay off ten-fold at home.

On those slightly stressful days when the grass looks a little greener and you feel like maybe you need a break, remember this: room service will never kiss you goodnight!

Room service will never provide you the love and comfort that you need, and impressing people that do not matter to you is useless in the end.

22. Hope and decisions

Making the decision to act is the most difficult part; the rest is just tenacity and perseverance. Fears are mere paper tigers. You can do absolutely anything that you decide to do. You can act to change and control your life.

When I was 25 years old, while waiting to pick up a friend at the airport in London, I had one of those life-changing experiences that you hear other people talk about. You know the kind that sneaks up on you unexpectedly.

Well, this one occurred a mere two feet away from me. Straining to locate my friend among the passengers coming out of the airport's exit, I noticed a man coming toward me carrying two light bags. He stopped right next to me to greet his family.

First, he motioned to his youngest son (maybe six years old) as he laid down his bags. They gave each other a long and movingly loving hug. As they separated enough to look in each other's face, I heard the father say, "It's so good to see you, son. I missed you so much!"

His son smiled somewhat shyly, diverted his eyes, and replied softly, "Me too, Dad!"

Then the man stood up, gazed in the eyes of his oldest son (maybe nine years old) and while cupping his son's face in his hands he said, "You're already quite the young man. I love you very much Sam!"

They too hugged a most loving, tender hug. His son said nothing. No reply was necessary.

While this was happening, a baby girl (perhaps one or one and a half) was squirming excitedly in her mother's arms, never once taking her little eyes off the wonderful sight of her returning father.

The man said, "Hello sweetie!" as he gently took the child from her mother. He quickly kissed her face all over and then held her close to his chest while rocking her from side to side. The little girl instantly relaxed and simply laid her head on his shoulder and remained motionless in total pure contentment.

After several moments, he handed his daughter to his oldest son and declared, "I've saved the best for last!"

He proceeded to give his wife the longest, most passionate kiss I ever remember seeing. He gazed into her eyes for several seconds and then quietly said, "I love you so much!"

They stared into each other's eyes, beaming big smiles at one another, while holding both hands. For an instant, they reminded me of newlyweds, but I knew by the age of their kids that they could not be. I puzzled about it for a moment, then realised how totally engrossed I was in the wonderful display of unconditional love not more than an arm's length away from me.

I suddenly felt uncomfortable, as if I were invading something sacred, but was amazed to hear my own voice nervously ask, "Wow! How long have you two been married?"

"Been together fourteen years total, married twelve of those." The man replied without breaking his gaze from his lovely wife's face.

"Well then, how long have you been away?" I asked.

The man finally looked at me, still beaming his joyous smile and told me, "Two whole days!"

Two days! I was stunned!

I was certain by the intensity of the greeting I just witnessed that he had been gone for at least several weeks, if not months, and I know my expression betrayed me. So, I said almost offhandedly, hoping to end my intrusion with some semblance of grace (and to get back to searching for my friend), "I hope my marriage is still that passionate after twelve years!"

The man suddenly stopped smiling. He looked me straight in the eye. With an intensity that burned right into my soul, he told me something that left me a different person.

He said, "Don't hope friend... decide."

Then he flashed me his wonderful smile again, shook my hand and said, "God bless!"

With that, he and his family turned and energetically strode away together.

I was still watching that special man and his exceptional family walk just out of sight when my friend came up to me and asked, "What are you looking at?" Without hesitating, and with a curious sense of certainty, I replied, "My future!"

23. The perception of a child

The perception of a child may irritate you, but if you are patient, it can lead you to an understanding of yourself. The world of a child is full of magic things. You should be patient with them so that your senses can grow sharper.

My mother used to tell me many stories when I was young. One of the most unforgettable stories that she told me was about the perception of a child. I guess she wanted me to be a great parent when I had my own children.

The story goes that some time ago, a man punished his three-year-old daughter for wasting a roll of gold wrapping paper. Money was tight in the family and he became infuriated when the child tried to decorate a box to put under the Christmas tree. Nevertheless, the little girl brought the gift to her father the next morning and said, "This is for you, daddy."

The man was embarrassed by his earlier overreaction, but his anger flared again when he found out the box was empty.

He yelled at her, saying, "Don't you know, when you give someone a present, there is supposed to be something inside?"

The little girl looked up at him with tears in her eyes and cried, "Oh, daddy, it's not empty at all. I blew kisses into the box. They're all for you, daddy."

The father was crushed. He put his arms around his little girl, and he begged for her forgiveness.

Only a short time later, an accident took the life of the child and mother. The father kept that gold box by his bed for many years and, whenever he was discouraged, he would take out an imaginary kiss and remember the love of the child who had put it there.

In a very real sense, each one of us, as human beings, have been given a gold container filled with unconditional love and kisses from our children, family members, friends. There is simply no other possession, anyone could hold, more precious than this.

24. Child's best day

Join your children's world when they are young, so that you are in their world when they become adults. For your children to turn out well, spend more time with them and not just spend money on them.

In his attic, an old man, tall and stooped, bent his great frame and made his way to a stack of boxes that sat near one of the little half-windows. Brushing aside a wisp of cobwebs, he tilted the top box toward the light and began to carefully lift out one old photograph album after another. Eyes, once bright but now dim, searched longingly for the source that had drawn him here.

It began with the fond recollection of the love of his life, long gone, and somewhere in these albums was a photo of her he hoped to rediscover. Silent as a mouse, he patiently opened the long buried treasures and soon was lost in a sea of memories. Although his world had not stopped spinning when his wife left it, the past was more alive in his heart than his present aloneness.

Setting aside one of the dusty albums, he pulled from the box what appeared to be a diary from his grown son's childhood. He could not recall ever having seen it before, or that his son had ever kept a diary.

Why did Elizabeth always save the children's old junk? He wondered, shaking his white head.

Opening the yellowed pages, he glanced over a short reading, and his lips curved in an unconscious smile. Even his eyes brightened as he read the words that spoke clear and sweet to his soul. It was the voice of the little boy who had grown up far too fast in this very house, and whose voice had grown fainter and fainter over the years. In the utter silence of the attic, the words of a guileless six-year-old worked their magic and carried the old man back to a time almost totally forgotten.

Entry after entry stirred a sentimental hunger in his heart like the longing a gardener feels in the winter for the fragrance of spring flowers. However, it was accompanied by the painful memory that his son's simple recollections of those days were far different from his own. But how different?

Reminded that he had kept a daily journal of his business activities over the years, he closed his son's journal and turned to leave, having forgotten the cherished photo that originally triggered his search.

Hunched over to keep from bumping his head on the rafters, the old man stepped to the wooden stairway and made his descent, then headed down a carpeted stairway that led to the den.

Opening a glass cabinet door, he reached in and pulled out an old business journal. Turning, he sat down at his desk and placed the two journals beside each other. His was leather-bound and engraved neatly with his name in gold, while his son's was tattered and the name Jimmy had been nearly scuffed from its surface.

He ran a long skinny finger over the letters, as though he could restore what had been worn away with time and use.

As he opened his diary, the old man's eyes fell upon an inscription that stood out because it was so brief in comparison to other days.

In his own neat handwriting were these words: **'Wasted the whole day fishing with Jimmy. I didn't catch a thing.'**

With a deep sigh and a shaking hand, he took Jimmy's journal and found the boy's entry for the same day, June 4. Large scrawling letters, pressed deeply into the paper, read: **'Went fishing with my Dad. Best day of my life.'**

...

I never remember the fancy toy that my father bought me when I was young. All my memories are about the time that we spent together playing a game of chess and drafts and the conversations that we had.

I also painfully remember the times that he stood me up and failed to come through with all his promises. These memories are stored directly in my tear ducts.

25. Wisdom

Wisdom is simply a lesson you learn and then apply it. It is that thing which makes you not only shine in the light, but glow in the dark. Guard your knowledge ferociously and use it when it is important.

Your life is bigger than any one experience. The wound that you faced as a child is no longer there. You know about wounds because of that experience. When you are wounded, turn your wounds into wisdom.

Learn to read signs. For example, when you are going off your course, the pain you face is a spur to action. It is not time to relax.

One music composer tells an inspiring story about his daughter. She was three and had just been released from a far-away hospital after a life threatening brain surgery. She was ready to take on the world again. He was happy just to have her back – this little "Miss Clean" (shaven head and hoop earrings)–and driving to their local mall for shopping to cheer her up. It was 'hanging out with dad day'.

He recalled her words as if it were yesterday, "Daddy, can I get a treat?"

As she was understandably spoilt, he replied: "Ok honey, but just one".

Her eyes beamed in anticipation of that something only she knew at the time.

They drove around to the new end of the mall on the normal seek-and-destroy mission of capturing a parking place. After all, it was Saturday. They landed a fair distance from their destination, and began walking hand-in-hand towards the entrance, her pace gaining momentum with each tiny step.

A few feet from the doors, she broke loose and ran hands-first into the thick wall of glass, trying with everything she had to swing the big doors open. No luck! With a little assistance, she 'did it' and tried the very same thing at the second set of doors.
It was then that he asked her what she wanted for her treat. Without hesitation, she matter-of-factly said, "An ice-cream cone from the ice-cream store". The goal was set and they were in the mall!

At the end of what was just an ordinary looking lane of retail chain outlets, she spied something new – a huge fountain, water shooting who knows how high into the air. She ran, he walked and they arrived at the spectacle at about the same time. The turbulent noise was almost deafening.

"Daddy, can I make a wish? Can I please make a wish?" she screamed as she jumped with the kind of pure joy we have all long since forgotten.

"Sure honey, but that will be *your one treat* you know," he explained firmly.

She agreed.

He fumbled around in his pocket and pulled out a pound coin. He placed it in her outstretched hand. She cupped it tightly, closed her eyes and grimaced, formulating her wish. He stared at that little scrunched-up face and said his own kind of prayer of thanks. He felt so blessed to still have this ball of energy in his life. Like a shooting star, she flung the coin into the foaming water and with it, her wish.

They happily continued their stroll into the familiar section of the mall. An eerie silence ensued, which he was uncomfortable with. He could not resist breaking it.

"Aren't you going to tell daddy what you wished for?"

She retorted, "I wished I could get an ice-cream cone".

He just about lost it at the moment and started laughing. Shoppers watched this lunatic laughing uncontrollably in the middle of a crowded mall. She got her wish and two treats.

Little did he know then that his beautiful little girl would soon embark on a long road of seizures, surgeries, special schools, medications and end up partially paralysed on her right side. She never learned to ride a bike.

Today, she is almost seventeen. She cannot use her right hand and walks with a noticeable limp. However, she has overcome what life seemed to so cruelly inflict on her. She was teased a lot and always struggled in school, both socially and academically, but each year she showed improvement.

Today, she is planning a career in early years education. With one year remaining in high school, they, one night not too long ago mapped out all the courses she would need to take in community college. It was her idea. She volunteers weekly at a local hospital, on the children's floor. She babysits a neighbour's child five days a week. On her own this year, she stood outside in line for four hours on a cold afternoon and enrolled herself, with her own babysitting money, into two courses she felt she would need for college.

You see, to her failure was never an option.

It would almost be redundant for me to explain why I wanted to share this story with you. This young lady is a very exceptional person and one that I admire and have learned a lot from.

It is my sincerest hope that her story will have even a momentary positive impact on you as a human being, friend, a sibling, a parent, a spouse or even, an entrepreneur.

As human beings, we deserve all the treats and the multitude of good things that life can offer us. We all have wishes, dreams and the power to make them reality. These are just truths of the universe.

We can wish for, and get, that ice-cream cone. In that process, we can create lasting relationships that help our families and relationships become strong.

26. Love

Life is precious. Family is precious. Handle both with care and spread love.

People that do the daring things in life, that make history and change the course of history have something inside of them. There is something that makes them unique. They make dramatic difference on the planet.

Something makes high achievers have the tenacity to make the kind of heat or fire they make. They face rejection, yet if you ask them why they do what they do, they will tell you, "It's worth it for me to do this."

They have found their pulse from somewhere. They have found something inside themselves that has given them strength to face the heat.

While others become cowards and run away, saying, "I can't do it," they have fire and desire that makes them say, "I can."

What gives us the courage and tenacity to stand up and the strength to break habits? What gives us the courage to have the dedication, determination to come back repeatedly when we fail?

It is worth it, when you love it.

Love will help you bridge many challenges and help you handle many obstacles. It is the love that you have for others, but mostly within yourself. Love will make you fight to mend your broken family. It will give you the passion to pursue your goals.

The story of Jack shows the power love.

Jack took a long look at his speedometer before slowing down: 73 miles in a 50 zone. This was the fourth time in as many months. How could a person be caught so often?

When his car had slowed to 10 miles an hour, Jack pulled over, but only partially. Let the police officer worry about the potential traffic hazard. Maybe some other car will tweak his backside with a mirror. The police officer was stepping out of his car, holding a big pad in his hand.

Jack saw Bob coming down to him. Bob from church? Jack sunk further into his trench coat. This was worse than the coming fine and points on his driving license. A policeman had caught someone from his own church, a man who happened to be a little eager to get home after a long day at the office, and someone he was about to play golf with tomorrow.

Jumping out of the car, he approached a man he saw every Sunday, a man he had never seen in uniform.

"Hi, Bob. Sorry meeting you like this," said Jack.

"Hello, Jack." No smile.

"Guess you caught me red-handed in a rush to see my wife and kids."

"Yeah, I guess." Bob seemed uncertain. Good.

"I've seen some long days at the office lately. I'm afraid I bent the rules a bit -just this once." Jack toed at a pebble on the pavement. "Diane said something about roast beef and potatoes tonight. Know what I mean?"

"I know what you mean. I also know that you have a reputation in our police station," said Bob.

Ouch! This was not going in the right direction. It was time to change tactics.

"What'd you clock me at?"

"Seventy. Would you sit back in your car please?"

"Now wait a minute here, Bob. I checked as soon as I saw you. I was barely nudging 65." The lie seemed to come easier with every ticket.

"Please, Jack, in the car."

Flustered, Jack hunched himself through the still-open door. Slamming it shut, he stared at the dashboard. He was in no rush to open the window. Minutes ticked by. Bob scribbled away on the pad. Why had he not asked for a driver's license?

A tap on the door jerked his head to the right. There was Bob, a folded paper in hand. Jack rolled down the window a mere two inches, just enough room for Bob to pass him the slip.

"Thanks." Jack could not quite keep the sneer out of his voice.

Bob returned to his police car without a word. Jack watched his retreat in the mirror. Jack unfolded the sheet of paper. How much was this one going to cost? Wait a minute. What was this? Some kind of joke? Certainly not a ticket. Jack began to read:

"Dear Jack,

> *Once upon a time, I had a daughter. She was six when killed by a car. You guessed it – a speeding driver. A fine and three months in jail, and the man was free. Free to hug his daughters – all three of them. I only had one, and I'm going to have to wait until Heaven before I can ever hug her again. A thousand times, I've tried to forgive that man. A thousand times, I thought I had. Maybe I did, but I need to do it again. Even now. Pray for me and be careful, Jack, my son is all I have left.*

Bob"

Jack turned around in time to see Bob's car pull away and head down the road. Jack watched until it disappeared. A full 15 minutes later, he too, pulled away and drove slowly home, praying for forgiveness and hugging a surprised wife and kids when he arrived.

Life is precious. Handle with care. Drive safely and carefully, and love your family, your friends and your relatives.

Love will give you the drive and energy that you need to keep going.

27. Choices

You are free to the choice that you want, but you are not free from the consequences of that choice. That choice you make today may break or make your family in future.

Any adventure that you choose to go on in life is going to be risky. Life itself is full of risks, but also many opportunities.

How do you make decisions about things that you are not sure about? How do you decide what to do when you have a vision, but the path is not very clear?

There is always more than one path to choose in any given situation. We often have to go into deep contemplated modes and engage in activities that support us in making decisions.

It has been said that on average, every adult makes around 35,000 choices every single day. Many of these decisions are conscious, but some are unconscious or automated based on your conditioning and habits formed over your entire life span.

These decisions can vary from meaningless choices like which socks to wear in the morning to life-changing choices like entering a relationship, breaking up a relationship with a toxic person, leaving a familial relationship nurtured over a long time.

The choices that we make every day determine who we will become and how we will live.

George Bernard Shaw once said, "Life isn't about finding yourself. Life is about creating yourself."

You create your life by the choices you make every single day. *The difference between a great life and a mediocre one is based on how many choices you make every day that are deliberate.*

How many brave choices do you make every day? How many choices you make are taking you in the direction of the life that you want? What if every decision you make was powerful? What if you were conscious of your decision making more often? Can you imagine what kind of life you would have in one, 5, 10 years time if every decision you made was on purpose?

What happens to me does not control my life. What I decide to do with what happens to me is what controls my life. My choices, decisions and actions control my life.

I decide if I will pick up the phone and make that call to mend my relationship with my mother. If I do not make that call, I must be prepared to face the consequences of making the decision not to call.

I decide if I will quit at the first sign of struggle, but I also decide if I will not. I have to live with the consequences of making either of those decisions.

Brothers Tino and Godfrey from my neighbourhood in Zimbabwe were both born in the early 1980s and grew up in a mostly poor neighbourhood in Harare. Both boys were well behaved in school and brought home great results on their report cards all through grade school.

However, coming from a poor family with eight children, money was always tight, so the boys often had to go without. In fact, things were so tight that the two growing boys were often hungry.

They did what many boys do when they are hungry and have no food–they stole. From the time they were five until they were well out of high school, the boys stole. They stole food from the cupboard in the middle of the night. They stole sweets and biscuits from the grocery store and they stole light bulbs from the hardware store near their house.

If it was not nailed down and was worth something Tino and Godfrey would find a way to steal it. They even stole money from their parents from time to time, even though their parents had very little money. More often than not, they stole to satisfy their hunger.

When it was time for Tino and Godfrey to attend high school, many things changed. It was during high school that something happened that made Tino decide to change his behaviour. At the end of his first year in high school, Tino had received three A's and three U's (ungraded) when he sat for his 'O' levels in June of that year—the first time he had failed anything in school. That failure shocked his system and he made up his mind to change. He would not make it to 'A' levels if he did not pass two more subjects including Maths and English.

Years later, Tino would recall that defining moment in his life with these words: "I sat outside my house at the beginning of that summer knowing that I was letting my chance slip away and was letting my family down. If I failed, I'd be just another high school dropout, hanging around the neighbourhood, and sliding into crime.

"At the time I didn't know my brother Godfrey would end up in prison or that my brother Chenge would die without having seen much of the world.

"I certainly didn't know what would happen to mum and dad. I only knew that I had to get out of there. I wanted no limitations. I wanted to be whatever a man could hope to be."

Tino's decision to change his behaviour was not an easy one. He took a lot of grief from his friends for choosing to excel in school. That decision to change took him in an entirely different direction from his brother Godfrey, who resisted changing his unproductive behaviour.

Tino went on to graduate pass his 'A' levels and graduate from University of Zimbabwe law school. For 15 years, he worked as a prosecutor, prosecuting murderers, drug dealers, thieves and corrupt officials. Today Tino is better known as Tinotenda, the top Harare lawyer.

What became of Tinotenda's brother, Godfrey? After high school Godfrey joined the Zimbabwe army briefly and left. He continued his pattern of anti-social behavior – hustling in the streets and stealing to support himself.

On October 19, 2018 Godfrey died at the age of 32 from AIDS. This caused a rift in the family, with members accusing Tino of witchcraft, saying he bewitched his brother so that he can be more successful than him. The family remains divided to this day with accusations running back and forth.

This story of triumph and tragedy serves to remind us that, when it is all said and done, who we are and what we become is determined by the choices we make.

We can choose to get better or we can choose to get bitter. Whether we make those choices to improve at age 16, like Tinotenda or at any other age, those choices have the power to dramatically increase our value in virtually everything we do.

That is what the saying 'change or be changed' is all about. Tinotenda changed. He changed from being a criminal to prosecuting criminals. He changed his attitude from being angry and sullen to being open and accepting. He changed from an underachiever to an honour student who took responsibility for his grades and his education and became a lawyer. He changed from a disillusioned teenager with low self-esteem to an optimistic young man determined to turn his dreams into reality.

His brother Godfrey, on the other hand, was changed. He was changed by grinding poverty. He was changed by illegal activity and finally, an insidious disease changed him.

Tinotenda made the tough choices. He made the changes in his life that helped him accomplish his dreams. His brother Godfrey, on the other hand, took the easy way out – or at least what he thought was the easy way out.

He kept hanging around the same group of loser friends. He kept practicing the same self-destructive habits. Because of the changes they did or did not make, both men chose their fates: Tinotenda chose to become a successful prosecutor and Godfrey chose to become just another sad story of the streets.

The sobering truth is, "Either way, you pay!" The truth is the price that Godfrey paid for refusing to change was much higher than the price that Tinotenda paid for seeking to change. I would like to think that Godfrey did not die in vain. I would like to think that by hearing this story, some people would finally understand the profound importance of making positive, productive changes in their lives.

When it's all said and done, you have a choice.

You can choose to become Godfrey or you can choose to become Tinotenda.

You can continue to do the things that will lead to frustration and unhappiness or you can make the changes that help you get what you want most out of life.

Do not choose to become like so many people who 'could have' become a millionaire or who 'could have' become happier or who 'could have' become healthier or who 'could have' contributed, but did not. Start making the changes you need to make *today* so that you can become the person you want to become *tomorrow*.

These changes will keep your family together. They will help stop unnecessary friction like we have seen in Tinotenda and Godfrey's household. Many problems that we face in our families are caused by the choices that siblings make. Those who lag behind blame those who make difficult decisions and advance themselves.

Make sure that in life you do not hide in the shadows or blend in with the background. Commit to becoming the best version of yourself.

Thinks about the compound effect of money. If you invest money into a high-interest return account, over time, you receive compound interest. That is interest on top of your interest.

This process is also true for the choices that you make every day–good choices and bad choices. We all know how quickly life can spiral out of control if we make many bad decisions, bad relationships, and bad choices of people to associate with.

This is also the case with good choices. You control your life better with good choices. If you are conscious of making powerful choices every day, those choices lead to better opportunities, best results and they compound on each other to bring a better life.

It takes character that most people do not have, to live life that most will never know. Decide to say no to average and to playing small. Commit to get some compound growth in your life. You deserve that.

28. A parent's pain

With age, and when you become a parent yourself, you will realise the pain you caused on the very same person you are taking for granted today—your parent. Do the best you can because this is probably the only chance you have to honour them.

It is a sad reality faced by many parents when their kids grow up and seem to take their existence for granted. While most parents understand that their adult children have busy professional and personal lives, they still feel the need to connect and still act as a family unit.

My aunt once told her family that she was going to stop all kitchen duties and general family maintenance until there was hard evidence of mutual respect and consideration within the home. A lot of tension had accumulated.

For years, it had been assumed that she would be the one to pick up the dropped socks, transfer the dirty tea and coffee cups from the table to the sink, extract the remote control from between the sofa cushions, replace the toilet roll, and buy all the stuff that was running out at home.

Everyone was amused when the dog was given a large bone. He played with it, licked it, carried it around, dropped it, nosed it, tasted it again, and backed away. The whole family watched, took photos, amused themselves and then drifted away, as the dog did, bored, ready for something new.

My aunt was building a family, a home filled with love and tradition and encouragement. Her husband, my uncle, paid no attention to the little things, with his growing career, each step forward creating another challenge to strive for, an accolade to win. Her children, my cousins, fabulous teenagers and young adults growing into themselves, living their unfettered lives, able to focus, to dream, to reach for the stars.

However, something went amiss—she became static. There was no more partnership. She was playing an assistant role. She became less the heart of the family, more the assumed caretaker. But here is the nub of it: they are supposed to be a family, a multidimensional unit that lives and loves in a mutually supportive way. *Everyone should step up and join in. She has a life to live as well.*

Healthy relationships require hard work, communication and compromise. The idea that if it is "meant to be" you will just sail along easily down the river to happy-ever-after is nonsense. While you will need to come to an agreement about certain things in your relationship, there will also be some things you should not budge on.

One of my cousins told me: "I can never date a bad communicator again. Trying to understand feelings, motives, everything with little hints and non-direct language made me lose my mind."

She added, "I can work through any sort of issue, but I'm not begging to find out what's on someone's mind. They should be an adult and speak up."."

29. Respect

You have to have self-respect and faith in yourself to cultivate the courage to commit to your endeavours even when no one, including family members, is by your side and neutralising the negative influences in your life.

We go through life taking in some things, in spite of those things draining our energy. There comes a time when we just have to draw the line and demand some respect.

You have to say, 'Enough is enough.' You have to do that for yourself. People around you who are not sensitive to who you are, will drain your energy and lead you on a destructive path. There are people that you love. They are the ones that you are vulnerable to. They are the ones that can get to you, and if they are insensitive, they will change you and soon enough you will be that vile, insensitive person like them. We mirror what we are accustomed to.

Therefore, you have to draw the line and demand respect, if it is not given to you.

Astrologer Theodore White said, "To go against the dominant thinking of your family, of most of the people you see every day, is perhaps the most difficult act of heroism you can perform."

When you start growing and changing the way you talk, walk and respond to things, people will put you on a guilt trip. They will use you and abuse you because they do not know how to deal with an empowered *you*. They want to see a weak *you*.

When this happens, you cannot leave your destiny to chance. You have to draw the line and demand respect. Do not go through life thinking that you are powerless. You are not powerless. You are powerful!

You direct the power in your life. Whatever is going on right now in your life is a duplication of your consciousness. It is a result of how you have decided to use your power. It is a result of how you have allowed certain people to treat you. That is not who you are. That is just a perverted use of your power that you are not satisfied with. You have the power to change that, wherever you are.

You can say, 'But you don't know what happened to me!' It does not matter what happened to you. All that matters is what you are going to do about it. That is all that matters. Whatever happened to you, you can allow it to destroy you or you can allow it to build you up.

The choice is yours.

Joan Didion writes, *'To free us from the expectation of others, to give us back to ourselves, there lies the great, singular power of self-respect.'* You have to have self-respect and faith in yourself to cultivate the courage to commit to your endeavours even when no one, including family members, is by your side and neutralising the negative influences in your life.

I grew up in Harare with Tariro. She now lives in the US. She has not spoken to her sister for two years because her sister 'does not know her boundaries and thinks that she is a parent.' They never really saw eye to eye about anything. When she was younger, it was just the simple stuff – the length of her skirt, how she chose to wear her hair or the boys she wanted to hang out with that caused problems between them.

But as she got older, she found that there was a lot more that they did not agree on–her choice of friends, who to date, political issues or how she chose to spend her weekends.

Moving to America totally broadened her outlook on the world. It has changed her opinion on many issues. She has met the most amazing people with the most extraordinarily and diverse experiences. Her circle of friends includes people with different beliefs and values and from different cultures.

Yet she still finds it hard to cope with her family situation. She finds it hard to deal with not being able to express her opinions as freely as she does when she is away from home.

Her sister still does not agree with her upfront attitude to life. While she is always out there trying to get people to take her and her beliefs and opinions seriously, her sister's attitude is, 'What's wrong with you? Why not just go with the flow?'

Tariro kept at it though. She used to ring home and tell her mother about a new project she had become involved with and even though she could just see her cringing on the other end of the phone line, she tried to remember why she was doing what she was doing or why she held the beliefs that she did.

Tariro really had to remind herself that it was fine to have the opinions that she did, but also that it was alright for her mother to have her viewpoint too. Respect is all that was needed.

The thing she loved about her friends was that they all respected each other's opinions. She had a chat to a friend about it and eventually realised that if she wanted her family to respect what she had to say, she had to try to respect their viewpoint too. As tough as it was, once she made an effort to respect their values and opinions, getting along with them has been a lot easier.

She stood up for herself and, rather than just taking things that come along her way with a hopeless demeanour, she confronted her problems head on and fought for what was hers.

James Allen, in his book entitled *A Man Thinketh*, beautifully compares the mind to a garden that is not tended to. It grows detrimental weeds. To grow beautiful flowers in a garden, it needs to be properly taken care of and regularly exposed to weed control techniques. This is where the phrase *'weed out toxic people from your life'* came from.

You do this by demanding respect, by drawing a bold red line that can be seen by people who try to take advantage of you. Then you will be able to tend your mind by carefully analysing the negative influences from your family and friends.

30. The family Whatsapp group

Do not be waylaid by a toxic family Whatsapp group. You fought hard to emerge as your own person in real life. Do not succumb to the new medium that replicates all the sad, toxic hierarchies of broken families. Walk out. Do it now.

With so many of us now constantly tethered to digital technology via our smartphones, tablets, and even watches, there is a huge experiment underway that we did not exactly sign up for. Companies like Facebook and Twitter are competing for our attention, and they are doing so in a very perceptive way, knowing the psychological buttons to push to keep us coming back for more.

There are people who say constant digital distractions are changing our social relationships for the worse— leaving many of us more scatterbrained, more prone to lapses in memory, and more anxious. Others say we are overreacting, like people in the past that panicked about new technologies such as the printing press or the radio.

Whatsapp is one such messaging application that has transformed our relationships. The family Whatsapp group is a modern phenomenon, borne out of a digital age that makes instant messaging one of the easiest ways to communicate. While group chats were once reserved for friends or work colleagues, the family Whatsapp group now takes the meme-filled, casual messaging service and uses it to keep up to date with family members. It removes the conventional effort of having to visit or ring relatives.

Many family Whatsapp groups have become a place where bigoted, thoughtless, vile, irrational, misogynistic ideas are posted by family members, causing a lot of tension. These posts cause distress and create many family problems. If you have a family Whatsapp group, you can guarantee there is a fringe group in existence, too, where the issues in the main group are discussed further by family members who are much closer to each other.

My fringe group is called "Family Moans". In this group, we comment on annoying things said in the main family Whatsapp group. Usually, it is how passive aggressive certain people have been, why someone has given himself or herself the role of parent when they are a sibling, an uncle or just another relative.

The family Whatsapp group is an obligation, much like sending your mother a Christmas present or being the first one to text your parent a happy birthday. It will never be as fun as the groups you have with your friends or work colleagues, but you can never get annoyed and leave the group, not if you want to be a good family member and avoid unnecessary family problems.

My friend, Patson says when their family Whatsapp group was first set up, he found it excruciatingly dull. It was often just his father and sister making arrangements, and everyone else quiet, wondering what the group was all about.

"Baba, I am just leaving now for Harare…"

"My Kenya airways flight lands at 2.30pm."

"OK, I will meet you at the airport."

"Have a great trip Patson."

Initially, Patson did what all good family members do and muted the group, rather than leave. However, when he noticed the messages swelling to 34, 52, 74 he thought maybe he should check in. Lo and behold, buried between all the mundane stuff, he found messages about new babies, news from his family in Zimbabwe and some nice old photographs his father had found of his mother.

Among the messages, he was stung by shame. He could no longer say he did not know about his cousin's engagement party. Part of him felt guilty that he had not attended the party, but his guilt did not last long. He remembered that no one had called him or invited him directly to the party and his shame turned to anger.

Feeling uncharitable, Patson questioned, in the family Whatsapp group, whether there was a way the family could make the group more relevant and not use it as a substitute for phone calls informing each other of important events. He learnt a big lesson as his cousin became defensive.

She blamed him for not congratulating her on her engagement to her Nigerian boyfriend and not 'liking' her pictures on Facebook and Instagram.

Today, they are no longer as close as they were before. In fact, they have spoken in six months and it looks like it will be a while before they make up.

Never *ever* question the content of the family Whatsapp group. If it is relevant to you, that is a great bonus. If it is not, be a good family member and shut up. Turn your notifications off and you are sure not to start unnecessary family feuds.

Another interesting story is about Maria. She moved to the United Kingdom around five years ago to study, but after meeting her boyfriend – who would later become her husband – she decided to stay. With relatives already in Europe and the United States, they decided to create a family Whatsapp group to keep in touch.

Admittedly, her relationship with her close relatives was a little fraught, due to their opposing political views. Maria would often lurk in the chat without sending any messages, trying to avoid conflict when others shared political views she disagreed with. Until one day, she saw something that she could not ignore.

"I normally keep quiet," Maria said.

"However, I couldn't keep my mouth shut after reading what they had said about Zimbabwe, and I called them out on it."

It did not go down well.

"My brother then told me to 'f* off', that he is ashamed of having me in 'their' family, which my sister agreed with and my cousins said nothing about," she continued.

"He then proceeded to remove me from the group, as he was the administrator."

This is how Maria felt when her brother used their disagreement to cut her out of their Whatsapp group.

"No one in my family got in contact with me at all, until my cousin contacted me about a week later regarding something else," says Maria.

"I tried to discuss it explaining I would quite like an apology. However, my cousin didn't really engage with that. He asked if I wanted to be added back and he could ask my brother to do so. I refused. I have not spoken with either my brother or my sister since, and my other relatives are pretending it never happened."

She adds that Whatsapp has caused a breakdown in communication with her relatives. "The relationship wasn't really great before, but now there is much less communication and I am no longer aware of what is happening in their lives. I'm still quite upset about it."

Clearly, Whatsapp groups can exacerbate existing family tensions, but for those who enjoy strong relationships with relatives they can be a great asset. For all the benefits of instant messaging, technology cannot solve family relationship issues and problems.

Reliance on digital communication can even leave us feeling less close to our family, if those chats start to replace meaningful real-world interactions.

I have, however, found our family Whatsapp group very useful in dealing with grief in the family. We have had a few deaths in the family—really close people. My cousin's mother passed away and that was a tragic moment for us in the family, but it was great because all of our cousins came together and we would check up on my cousin on the group chat and also outside of Whatsapp. It was a great asset.

However, if your family Whatsapp group has become toxic, recondition your mind and be bold enough to leave. You may leave the family group but the family will never leave you. It is your family after all.

Once you stop reading the offensive Whatsapp forwards of your family members, you will be able to recover your relationships with individual relatives. You will no longer associate the scientist in your family with the unscientific post she sent about how coloured candles defeat Coronavirus.

You will not be forced to remember the hateful and offensive post your sister forwarded to the group. You will forget how gullible your uncle is, the one who was once your childhood hero.

You will not be offended by your aunt sharing the same conspiracy theory about how Bill Gates is trying to control the world by finding a vaccine for Covid19.

Leaving the family Whatsapp group is an act of calmness. It is an act of self-preservation and family preservation.

Leaving means you can make your choices and feel your feelings without imposing them on anyone else. It means you are creating space for your own self, and not engaging in mindless family issues.

You should resist the easy temptation to turn your frustration into rage towards your own family members. Choose not to fritter away your energy where it will solve no problems and definitely create a few useless ones. Truly, people are much more than what they post or like on social media.

31. Characters in family Whatsapp groups

The last chapter discussed the role of the Whatsapp family group. To truly understand the challenges that the group imposes on individual family members, it is important to know the different characters within the group and find ways to deal with them when there is potential for problems.

Family Whatsapp groups are like the families: Witty, funny, useful, annoying, supportive, loving, nagging, prone to misunderstandings and moments of occasional hilarity. They are always there, whether you want to be part of them or not. You can mute them any time you like, the same way you can stay away from certain family functions.

Here are some of the distinct types of characters you will find in every group.

The bully

Every group has its bully. They are typically aggressive and combative, always looking to liven things up when the group is too silent. The bully will wake everyone up with a political message and dare them to challenge him. Whenever there is a discussion within the group, the bully will talk over everyone else.

The bully is often bossy and rude, dismissing others because he or she knows best. The bully is typically the cause of drama and fights within the family groups and the cause of many problems within the family at large.

The whiner

The way groups are structured means conversation drifts around various random topics. Not all of the topics will be relevant to every group member. As such, there is often one member of the group whose contributions consist almost entirely of complaints. When the group is too active, they will complain about the many notifications and how they are failing to keep up with them.

When it goes too silent, they are the first to ask members to *changamuka*. On the personal front, they never hesitate to spill their problems in the group. On a Monday morning they say things like, "This economy is killing us." The first place they go to complain about anything political is not the politician's Twitter page, but the family group, where they want their pain to be felt more deeply.

Dim-witted

There is always that one person who shows up to a problematic discussion three hours after it has cooled down. Whether it is because they are not constantly online or because their notifications do not work, they come late to the discussion, commenting on the explosive topic after everyone has moved on.

Their jokes and forwarded memes are a few months old, meaning most people have already seen them, and can only respond with a sympathetic lol! Then there is the unfortunate member who just cannot figure out this Whatsapp business, so the app keeps uninstalling. They are always leaving and re-joining the group to the annoyance of everyone else.

The black sheep

Often, the black sheep of the family does not even know their status. It could be cousin David and his inability to keep a girlfriend. Other family members peel away from the main group and form side groups, or what I called 'fringe groups' in the last chapter, where they discuss how to deal with the black sheep.

Members of the fringe group discuss whether they should invite him or her to the upcoming function or not. They worry that the black sheep could do something inappropriate. Ironically, this person is usually not bothered by their 'condition'. They can say the most inappropriate thing in the group, not get a response, and still continue posting.

The braggart

The rich also find themselves in family Whatsapp groups. They rarely have time to engage in the groups, but when they *drop by,* they never fail to remind the rest of the family just how successful they are. They post photos of their new car, trips to foreign lands and their children's achievements. They brag how successful their children are and how they are just as smart as they are. In the event of a fundraising, the braggart makes a hefty contribution to show others 'how it should be done'. They forget that not everyone is as rich as them.

The church mouse

The same quiet, shy people who sit at the back during family gatherings also take a back seat in the Whatsapp group. They operate on the *'maziso'* principle. They see it all, but they say nothing. Even when the group erupts into chaos with insults flying left, right and centre, they keep quiet, watching and shaking their heads. Usually, family groups tend to keep their membership tight, only allowing immediate family members in.

When someone sneaks in their wife or husband, that in-law lives like a new student in class, speaking only when spoken to. These people are not to be taken lightly. They usually have explosive gossip on the family, behind the scenes. They record everything and are often the cause of many family problems. They can detonate when pushed against the wall.

The fighter

The fighter is the loose cannon of the family. They are fearless and bold, always at the heart of fights and arguments. In the heat of battle, they will gladly reveal whose wife likes smiling suggestively at men in the family. They are very familiar with family dynamics and family fights, so they throw themselves into every argument armed to the teeth with history and fact.

Anything can set them off, even a single mention of a past family event. They are often the administrator of the group, and if they are not, the administrator will not dare to evict them from the group.

Stingy

Most family Whatsapp groups are started around a family function or event, for example a wedding, a death in the family or a party. Funerals, weddings and graduation ceremonies all need planning, which necessitates the formation of the group.

Naturally, the discussion often turns to making contributions. It is in these moments that the true nature of family members is revealed. Pay attention the next time someone mentions contributing money.

If you look keenly, you will see the stingy ones backing away slowly, and then just going quiet, in spite of being major contributors to issues not related to money. These members will never give out a single penny, no matter what it is for. It is not that they do not have the money; they are just naturally tight-fisted or think their money is worth more than that of others.

These family group members will contribute to their friend's birthday party, but will never contribute anything to a family function. They are also quick to complain if family members do not support them in their endeavours.

Broke

Contrary to the stingy members, the real heroes of the family Whatsapp groups are the perpetually broke members. Their wallets are always empty. Everyone understands their situation, so when something comes up, they sneak away into sub-groups to discuss how they can help their family member. No one asks anything of them. If they sense that they are feeling pressured, they suggest that the contributions be carried out without posting to the family Whatsapp group.

The pastor

Every group has that member who will not rest until everyone accepts Christ as their personal saviour. It is often everyone's favourite aunt, who goes to church every day and is part of three other Whatsapp prayer groups.

Their contribution to the group varies between posting long, copied-and-pasted messages meant to shame group members into salvation, and quietly judging them for their heathen ways. They quote scriptures at will, much to the annoyance of the other family members.

When side groups are formed, a big part of their appeal is that people can say whatever they want without the wrath of God descending on them.

32. Conclusion

Are you going through family problems? Are growing through them? Are you becoming better and wiser because of them, or mean and obnoxious because of them?

Family problems are not going to leave you until you grow through them. Until you handle your family problems with grace, they will stay in your face.

Do not get stuck. Do not wallow in family problems until they start affecting you psychologically. When you are stuck, you are wounded so badly that you take your pain to other people who did not cause that pain in the first place.

Recondition your mind, take action and change your life. Only then can you resolve family problems that are a noose on your neck.

You can resolve your family problems by *changing your mindset, changing your belief system*, changing the *words they use in conversations*. You have to *stop making excuses* about not making decisions and taking action.

You have to *become fearless*, and to *find and pursue your true purpose in life*.

Bonus chapters

33. Your choice, your life

When things go wrong, do not go with them. Make sure you fail your way to success by programming yourself to success. You have to be hungry all the time, so die hungry.

I t is easy to forget how blessed you are when you surround yourself with toxic people. It is easy to forget how capable you are, how kind you are and how good life is. It is also easy to forget all of your qualities when you surround yourself with the wrong people. When you do not have a mind of your own, you have no choices and your voice does not matter.

If you hang around people who are sick all the time, common sense will tell you that it is only a matter of time before you get sick. They infect you with their negativity and make you sick with negativity. They make you sick of everything, including yourself and the life that you are living. Soon enough you start living a small life and you cannot fit a big dream into a small life!

I like the saying that, "Always strive to get to the top of life because it's the bottom that is overcrowded." Give yourself permission to go forward, to test yourself, to challenge yourself. The reason you are here on earth is that there is something in you that says 'I can do more.' The life you have today cannot be the totality of your existence. Otherwise, why do you get up every day, get dressed, go to work, attend some training, and educate yourself more? *You have not yet peaked your life yet.*

A lady I worked with at the London Borough of Kensington and Chelsea back in the 1990s told me that she spent her life thinking that if she just did x, y, z, she could get her fiancé to realise that he was being toxic. She thought that he would see the light and their life would turn around.

She invested thousands of pounds in an attempt to prove that she could turn him around and get him to stop being self-destructive and destructive to the people around him. She took him to counselling, couples' seminars, holidays and sporting events, just to show him a different lifestyle. She said that, in the end, every single pound was a total waste.

Each instance was a failure. Whenever she tried to show him a different life, he abused that space. She introduced him to her family, but it was a disaster. Toxic people leak out and infect everyone around them, resulting in confusion and chaos. In this particular situation, the gossip and intrigue were unstoppable. There was endless conflict and a sense of being knocked off your game repeatedly.

If you want to advance your life, you have a choice to make. You can choose to live your life according to your standards or according to the standards of your toxic fiancé or family members. If the people you are hanging around with by choice are not making you better, they are making you worse.

The people around you should be making you feel better about life no matter what is going on in that life. Take a moment to think about the people that you spend your time with. How are they making you feel?

Motivational speaker, Jim Rohn, says, *"You're the average of the five people spend the most time with."* There is also the "show me your friends and I'll show you your future" derivative. Whichever you have heard, the intent is the same. Audit the people around you. Make sure that you are spending time with people who are in line with what you want for your own life (preferably people "better" than you, so that you raise your average).

I will add another derivative to this. You are the average of all the people who surround you. Look around and make sure you are in the right surroundings.

Who are the people surrounding you?

Do you want to be the average of their kindness?

The average of their integrity?

The average of their desire to improve?

The average of who they are as complete human beings?

Alternatively, can you do better? Do you know if you are capable of doing better? If not, it is time to make a change. To make real change, you have to think beyond just the people you hang around. You have to think about the books you read, the TV you watch or do not watch, the people you listen to, and the things you choose to believe.

Whatever you consume will consume you. Whatever you allow in your life becomes your life. You have to be ruthless with everything and everyone you allow in your life.

If you are hanging with people who have no standards, you have no standards. If you want to raise the level of your life, raise your standards and increase the quality of the people you spend time with—whether they are family, friends, acquaintances or colleagues. **It is your choice. This is your life. You set the standards.**

It is fine to live a life that people do not understand. It is fine to live a life that your family members or childhood friends do not understand. **This is your life. You set the standards.** It is not for them to understand it. It is for you to thrive and to live to your fullest so that you can achieve you goals and ambitions.

If you choose to live with people with no morals, eventually you will have no morals. If you choose to hang around family members who have no respect, what does that say about you?

If you choose to hang around people who are against your values, then you too are going against your values. If you choose to hang around with drifters, it is only a matter of time before you start drifting.

If you hang around people with no ambition and no desire to improve themselves, you have no chance of improving yourself. You must choose better! You have to surround yourself with people who make you better and hold you to higher standards.

You want to go to your grave knowing that you always did what was right, not what was easy or pleasing to the majority. You do not want to have spent your life doing what fit in with everyone else's comfort. You cannot spend time with toxic, low-value people and expect to live a great life.

It is not going to be easy to get rid of toxic people, especially if they are family members. It is a hard decision, but you will have to make it. How can you choose who to spend *more time with*, *little time with*, and *no time with*? Would you like to spend your time pleasing people at your expense, falling in line, never standing up for what you know is right for you? If you do, then know that you will never live your fullest life. However, if you want a fuller, more fulfilling life, you have to know how to recognise and deal with toxic people.

How then do you recognise and then deal with toxic family members?

34. Tools for dealing with toxic people

This is your life. Every breath you waste on toxic people is a breath you cannot get back.

Recognising toxic people is not easy. Even after you have recognised them, dealing with them is even harder, especially if they are family members.

My uncle was an abusive narcissist. My aunt and him are now divorced. She said that she learnt a number of things from him. The biggest lesson, she said, was being able to recognise a toxic person from far away.

The first telltale sign (from her experience) was that you begin to question reality.

She said, "First, you are asked to change small things about yourself and then increasingly larger things. No matter what you give the person, they will always be disappointed and you are never quite good enough."

She added, "I would try to reason with him and to explain why I wanted to continue to wear blue or why I wanted to keep my hair short, or have weave or braids. I had to explain why I didn't think I was such a bad wife or that my mother wasn't actually as bad as he was making her out to be."

She finally found the courage to cut him off, but after 20 difficult years.

My aunt's problem was that she engaged with his toxicity as if it was valid. If you give any validity to a toxic person, that person has got you because what they want is for you to play according to their rules. They want to be able to change the rules whenever they want with no repercussions.

Once you recognise that someone has these tendencies, you should be determined to show them the road. They need healing in a different space and not with you. The problem with my aunt was that she was trying to teach a toxic person to be non-toxic. That is like teaching someone to fly. You cannot do it and it does not matter how much you want to, it will never work.

If you feel like you have people around you that do not support you, or you are in a relationship with someone that does not value your dreams, or friends that are constantly degrading you, there is only one action to take: cut off ties and do not look back. If it is a family member, keep them at as far a distance as possible.

This is your life. Every breath you waste on toxic people is a breath you cannot get back.

So how do you deal with toxic people?

Toxic is a word that brings to mind something that is poisonous. There are three different stages to deal with toxic family members. The stages stem from the question: *What happens when you are exposed to something toxic?*

The stages are: rinsing, ingesting and prevention.

Stage 1: Rinsing of toxicity

Rinsing involves three strategies: *self-care, debriefing,* and *having the right perspective.*

Toxic stuff causes a sting, and when that happens, the first thing you do is to rinse with water or some medical substance. This helps diffuse, dilute or cleanse the pain to minimise the initial effects of the toxic exposure. *This is self-care.*

In a relationship setting, the initial sting can be a brusher like harsh words, physical violence, emotional abuse, or financial abuse. This initial sting can be diffused or diluted through self-care or taking care of yourself in a way that fortifies you against these *brushers*. For example, getting enough sleep, feeding yourself well and getting enough exercise puts you in the right mental state to deal with rubbish. All these elements of self-care help to dilute the initial effects of having a toxic relationship or interaction with a family member.

Another very important strategy that can help deal with toxic family members is *debriefing*. It is a strategy that can be used to deal with a toxic family member, a co-worker or someone who has caused you some pain. Debriefing simply means 'talking it through with that someone,' telling them what happened. This helps to dilute the sting a little bit, but only initially, and some of the toxic long term effects of that interaction.

A third strategy is *perspective*. Keep everything, including the family problem, in perspective. Ask yourself the question: *How big of a deal is it really?* In the moment, some family problems feel huge, but after taking a high perspective, a higher altitude view of the problem, it may start to shrink down.

The problem may be important to you, but in the grand scheme of things, it is probably not that big of a deal. Keeping that kind of a perspective helps to alleviate some of that initial sting or problem with a family member.

Stage 2: Ingestion of toxicity

The second stage is when you have ingested some toxic material and maybe it is starting to have some effect, or maybe it is a longer-term thing that you are dealing with. At this stage, you want to purge, antidote, counteract or remove, if possible, the poison or the toxin from our system. If that relates to family relationships, we cannot remove them from our lives, so we have to recondition our mind to see things differently.

We take something that has happened back in time and rework it to a point where it is not having the same toxic effect in our lives anymore. This book aims to help with that, by giving real life examples.

Stage 3: Prevention

The third strategy to deal with poisons or toxins is *prevention*. This can also be called *precaution, protection* or *avoidance* of future or further contact with that toxin or poison. When you apply that to relationships, you have to figure out what you can do to protect yourself in the future from experiencing that toxic interaction.

One of the things we can do is for you to set appropriate boundaries and limits. Nobody else is going to do this for you, so it is important that you identify what is alright and what is not alright; what you will allow, what you will not allow; what positions you are willing to put yourself in, versus what positions you are not going to get into. *You get to set these limits. Setting them appropriately and assertively is a great way to protect yourself from future toxic exposure, future abuse and pain.*

You have to use assertive communication. *This should not be confused with aggressive communication. They are not the same thing.* Being assertive is often confused with meanness, but it is not. Just use assertive communication to express your views and your boundaries so that you are not misconstrued or stung by the same toxic elements again.

For example, tell your cousin who tried to chat you up or an uncle who made an inappropriate, crude or rude joke that you will not tolerate that sort of behaviour again. This way, you are sending a clear message about the boundaries that you are willing to accept.

The other way to protect yourself from toxic people is to *opt out* of situations. It is your choice to opt out and you should never feel guilty. However, make sure you only opt out when it is appropriate and when it makes sense. You should never feel guilty to opt out of an event, an interaction or a conversation, if it is not going well for you. If the conversation or event is toxic, opting out is the way to protect yourself from the effects.

You can use a statement like, "This conversation is not serving me well right now!" and then opt out.

This should not be confused with avoiding people, but building and enhancing relationships that are healthy, affirming, and positive. You opt out to recondition, to change your way of thinking. Opting out helps draw you out of toxic exposure.

About the Author

Itayi Garande is a lawyer and award-winning author who has written the Amazon No. 1 Best Sellers, *Reconditioning: Change your life in one minute* and *Shattered Heart: Overcoming Death, Loss, Breakup and Separation.*

He has a book publishing company called Dean Thompson Publishing and has helped many authors to publish their books, especially on domestic abuse and domestic violence. He also runs an employment agency in Southend-on-Sea, specialising in health and social care. He places nurses, social workers and carers in NHS, local council organisations and the private sector.

He specialises in international commercial law, and immigration and asylum law. He is a member of the Law Society of England and Wales and the Bar Association and the United Kingdom's Bar Council.

He is a consultant Business Analysts and Project Manager who has worked in various public and private sector companies. He is a Certified Business Analyst, Certified Scrum Master (CSM®) and holds a CBAP (Certified Business Analysis Professional) qualification – the highest business analysis certification.

Itayi is a qualified gemmologist specialising in diamonds and other precious minerals and is a member of the Gemological Institute of America (GIA™). He is a certified diamond valuer with certificates in Diamonds and Diamond Grading and in 2014 became an Accredited Jewellery Professional (AJP) of GIA™. Through his company, Simba Resources, he manages contracts for African gold and diamond producers who trade with Western, Asian and Latin American organisational buyers. He is passionate about travel, motivational writer, speaker and blogger. He has two children with his wife Rose and they live in Essex, United Kingdom.

Contact

For speaking engagements, magazine and book contributions, contact Itayi Garande at:

itayi@itayigarande.com
www.itayigarande.com